PHILIP'S

Cycle TOURS

Cumbria and the Lakes

Nick Cotton

First published in 2002 by
Philip's, a division of
Octopus Publishing Group Ltd
2-4 Heron Quays
London E14 4JP

First edition 2002
First impression 2002

Based on the original Ordnance Survey Cycle Tours series
first published by Philip's and Ordnance Survey®.

ISBN 0-540-08203-1

The route maps in this book are reproduced from
Ordnance Survey® Landranger® mapping.

Text and compilation copyright © Philip's 2002

Photographic acknowledgements

AA Photo Library 13, 73 top • E A Bowness 103, 111 • Reed
International Books (John Freeman) 95 • B & S Thomlinson 7,
19, 25, 43, 49 • Judy Todd 37, 67 • Douglas Wood 107

Contents

Abbreviations and symbols

Directions

L	left
R	right
LH	left-hand
RH	right-hand
SA	straight ahead or straight across
T-j	T-junction, a junction where you have to give way
X-roads	crossroads, a junction where you may or may not have to give way
'Placename 2'	words in quotation marks are those that appear on signposts; the numbers indicate distance in miles unless stated otherwise

Distance and grade

The number of drink bottles indicates the grade:

Easy

Moderate

Strenuous

The grade is based on the amount of climbing involved.

Refreshments

Pubs and teashops on or near the route are listed. The tankard ♥ symbols indicate pubs particularly liked by the author.

Page diagrams

The page diagrams on the introductory pages show how the map pages have been laid out, how they overlap and if any inset maps have been used.

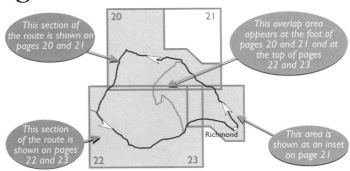

This section of the route is shown on pages 20 and 21

This overlap area appears at the foot of pages 20 and 21 and at the top of pages 22 and 23

This section of the route is shown on pages 22 and 23

Richmond

This area is shown as an inset on page 21

Cross-profiles

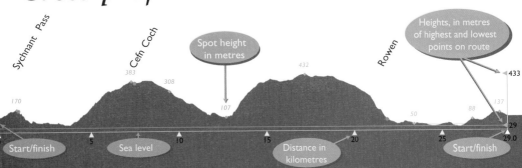

Sychnant Pass

Cefn Coch

Spot height in metres

Rowen

Heights, in metres of highest and lowest points on route

383
308
432
433

170
107
50
88
137
29

Start/finish

Sea level

Distance in kilometres

Start/finish

Legend to 1:50 000 maps

Roads and paths

Motorway

Service area   M 5   Elevated

Junction number 20

Motorway under construction

Trunk road

Unfenced   Footbridge

A 46 (T)

Main road

Dual carriageway

A 420

Main road under construction

Secondary road

B 4348

Narrow road with passing places

A 855   B 885

Road generally more than 4 m wide

Bridge

Road generally less than 4 m wide

Other road, drive or track

Path

Gradient: 1 in 5 and steeper, 1 in 7 to 1 in 5

Gates   Road tunnel

Passenger ferry   Vehicle ferry

Ferry P   Ferry V

Public rights of way (Not applicable to Scotland)

- Footpath
- Bridleway
- Road used as a public path
- Byway open to all traffic

Danger Area   Firing and test ranges in the area. Danger! Observe warning notices

Tourist information

ℹ ℹ	Information centre, all year / seasonal
P	Parking
✕	Picnic site
☆	Viewpoint
⋀	Camp site
⌖	Caravan site
▲	Youth hostel
	Selected places of tourist interest
✆	Public telephone
✆	Motoring organisation telephone
⌐	Golf course or link
PC	Public convenience (in rural areas)

Railways

	Track: multiple or single
	Track: narrow gauge
	Bridges, footpath
	Tunnel
	Viaduct
	Freight line, siding or tramway
a b	Station, (a) principal, (b) closed to passengers
LC	Level crossing
	Embankment
	Cutting

Rock features

outcrop

650

cliff

600

scree

Public rights of way indicated by these symbols have been derived from Definitive Maps as amended by the latest enactments or instruments held by Ordnance Survey and are shown subject to the limitations imposed by the scale of mapping. Further information may be obtained from the appropriate County or London Borough Council

The representation of this map of any other road, track or path is no evidence of the existence of a right of way.

◆ ◆ ◆	National Trail, Long Distance Route, selected recreational paths
● ● ●	National/Regional Cycle Network
— — —	Surfaced cycle route

Water features

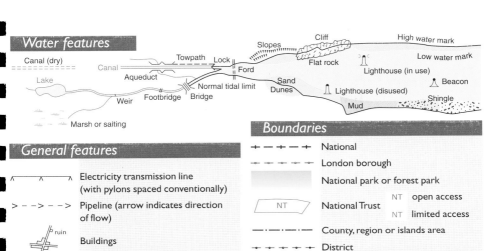

Canal (dry)
Canal
Lake
Aqueduct
Towpath
Lock
Ford
Weir
Footbridge
Bridge
Normal tidal limit
Marsh or salting

Slopes
Cliff
High water mark
Flat rock
Low water mark
Sand
Dunes
Lighthouse (in use)
Lighthouse (disused)
Beacon
Shingle
Mud

General features

⋀——⋀——⋀	Electricity transmission line (with pylons spaced conventionally)
> – –> – –>	Pipeline (arrow indicates direction of flow)
	Buildings
	Public buildings (selected)
	Bus or coach station
	Coniferous wood
	Non-coniferous wood
	Mixed wood
	Orchard
	Park or ornamental grounds
	Quarry
	Spoil heap, refuse tip or dump
	Radio or TV mast
	Church or chapel with tower
	Church or chapel with spire
+	Church or chapel without tower or spire
∘	Chimney or tower
	Glasshouse
	Graticule intersection at 5' intervals
Ⓗ	Heliport
△	Triangulation pillar
	Windmill with or without sails
	Windpump

Boundaries

+— —+— —+	National
–∘–∘–∘–∘–∘–	London borough
	National park or forest park
NT	National Trust
—·——·——·—	County, region or islands area
–+–+–+–+–+–	District

NT	open access
NT	limited access

Abbreviations

P	Post office
PH	Public house
MS	Milestone
MP	Milepost
CH	Clubhouse
PC	Public convenience (in rural areas)
TH	Town hall, guildhall or equivalent
CG	Coastguard

Antiquities

VILLA	Roman
Castle	Non-Roman
⤬	Battlefield (with date)
☆	Tumulus
+	Position of antiquity which cannot be drawn to scale
ℳ	Ancient monuments and historic buildings in the care of the Secretaries of State for the Environment, for Scotland and for Wales and that are open to the public

Heights

50	Contours are at 10 metres vertical interval
·144	Heights are to the nearest metre above mean sea level

Heights shown close to a triangulation pillar refer to the station height at ground level and not necessarily to the summit

North from Brampton to Bewcastle and the valleys of the Black and White Lyne

Start

Tourist Information Centre, Brampton

P Just off Front Street (on which the Tourist Information Centre is located) up Gelt Street then 1st left

Distance and grade

48 km (30 miles)
Moderate

Terrain

Generally open, undulating country with large tracts of forestry land in the distance. Four climbs of between 70 and 91 m (230 and 300 feet) on the outward section.

In years gone by, this would have been lawless country close to the border between England and Scotland and subject to frequent raids from marauding cattle-rustlers. The ride stays on open country with fine views, avoiding the dense forestry plantations lying to the east and north. There is a feeling of gentle neglect to the tumble-down stone walls and green pastures beneath the rounded grassy slopes of The Beacon and Grey Hill. Unusual buildings along the route include the Priory at Lanercost, Askerton Castle (which is really just a farm), the castle and church at Bewcastle, and not least, the unlikely situated Lime Kiln Inn. Several tributaries of the River Lyne, which empties its water into the Solway Firth north of Carlisle, are crossed at the northern end of the route before the ride turns south. Any signpost with a collection of such curious names as Kinkry Hill, Cumcrook and Dodgsonford invites exploration and the ford crossing of the Black Lyne is one of the memorable moments of the ride. After a few quiet miles on roads through Boltonfellend and Hethersgill, the main A6071 is joined for 5 km (3 miles) to return to the start.

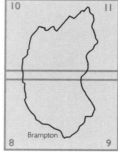

Brampton   Lanercost   Banks   Askerton Castle   Tower Brae   Bewcastle

3 climbs of between 45 and 61 m (150 and 200 feet) on the return. Highest point – 228 m (750 ft) just north of Bewcastle. Lowest point – 30 m (100 ft) at the crossing of the River Irthing west of Brampton

Nearest railway

Brampton Station lies 3 km (2 miles) south-east of Brampton

Refreshments

Plenty of choice in **Brampton** *Appleby Bridge Inn PH,* **Lanercost** *Lime Kiln Inn PH,* **Bewcastle** *Pointers Dog Inn PH,* **Bolton Fell End**

Places of interest

Brampton 1
Market town with cobbled streets and slate-roofed brick buildings where the octagonal Moot Hall, built in 1817, has clock tower cum belfry, external staircases and iron stocks. One of the shops in High Cross Street was Bonnie Prince Charlie's headquarters in 1745

Lanercost 3
The Priory was founded in 1166, damaged by Scottish raiders in the 13th and 14th centuries, and abandoned in 1536 during the Dissolution of the Monasteries. The aisle has windows by Victorian artists, William Morris and Edward Burne-Jones

Naworth Castle (just off the route) 3
A border stronghold built in 1335, turned into a mansion in the 17th century and now the home of the Earl of Carlisle

Bewcastle 5
Village near to the 6-acre site of a Roman fort, an outpost of Hadrian's Wall. The shaft of a 1300 year old cross in the church yard, one of the finest Anglo-Saxon crosses in Europe, has runic inscriptions and carvings of figures

◀ *Lanercost Bridge*

Kinkry Hill   Black Lyne   Boltonfellend   Hethersgill   Newtown   River Irthing

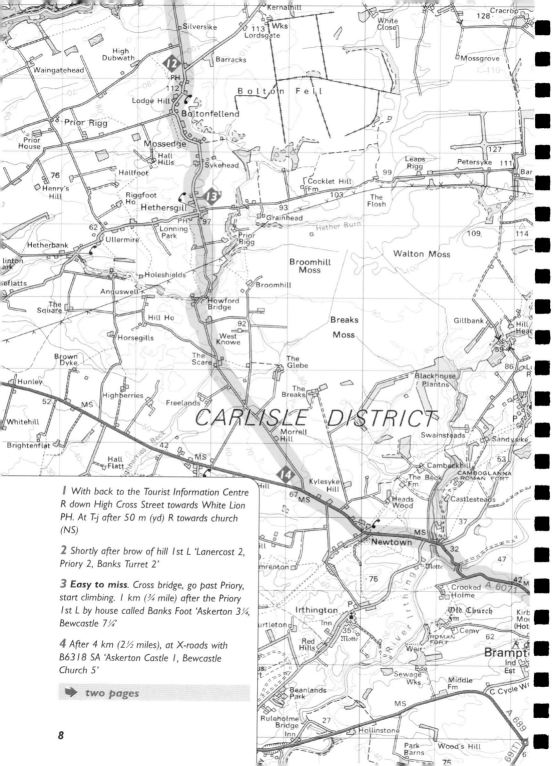

1 With back to the Tourist Information Centre R down High Cross Street towards White Lion PH. At T-j after 50 m (yd) R towards church (NS)

2 Shortly after brow of hill 1st L 'Lanercost 2, Priory 2, Banks Turret 2'

3 *Easy to miss.* Cross bridge, go past Priory, start climbing. 1 km (¾ mile) after the Priory 1st L by house called Banks Foot 'Askerton 3¼, Bewcastle 7¼'

4 After 4 km (2½ miles), at X-roads with B6318 SA 'Askerton Castle 1, Bewcastle Church 5'

➡ two pages

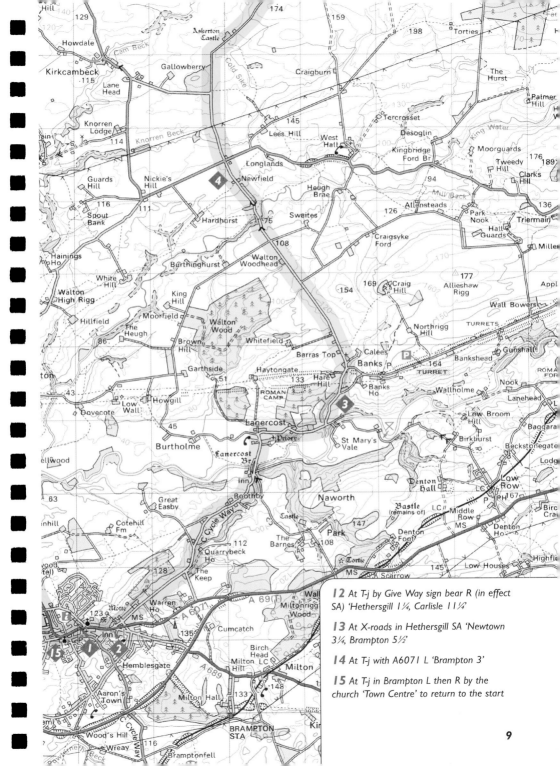

12 At T-j by Give Way sign bear R (in effect SA) 'Hethersgill 1¼, Carlisle 11¼'

13 At X-roads in Hethersgill SA 'Newtown 3¼, Brampton 5½'

14 At T-j with A6071 L 'Brampton 3'

15 At T-j in Brampton L then R by the church 'Town Centre' to return to the start

9

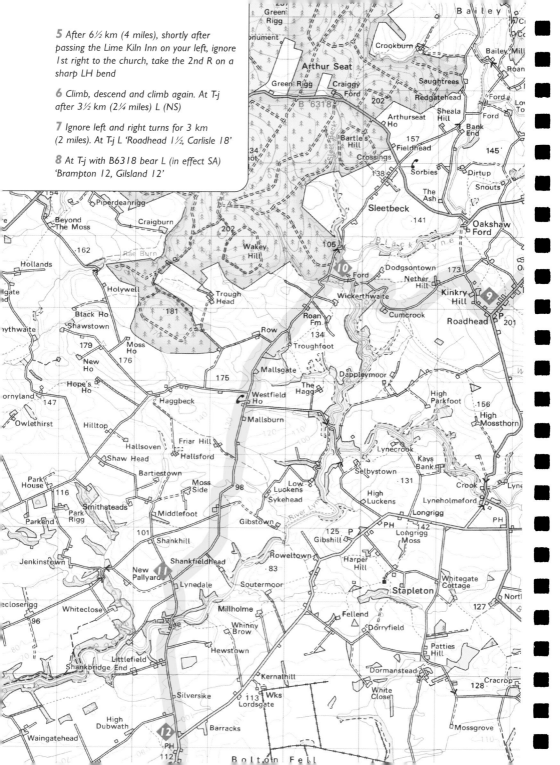

5 After 6½ km (4 miles), shortly after passing the Lime Kiln Inn on your left, ignore 1st right to the church, take the 2nd R on a sharp LH bend

6 Climb, descend and climb again. At T-j after 3½ km (2¼ miles) L (NS)

7 Ignore left and right turns for 3 km (2 miles). At T-j L 'Roadhead 1½, Carlisle 18'

8 At T-j with B6318 bear L (in effect SA) 'Brampton 12, Gilsland 12'

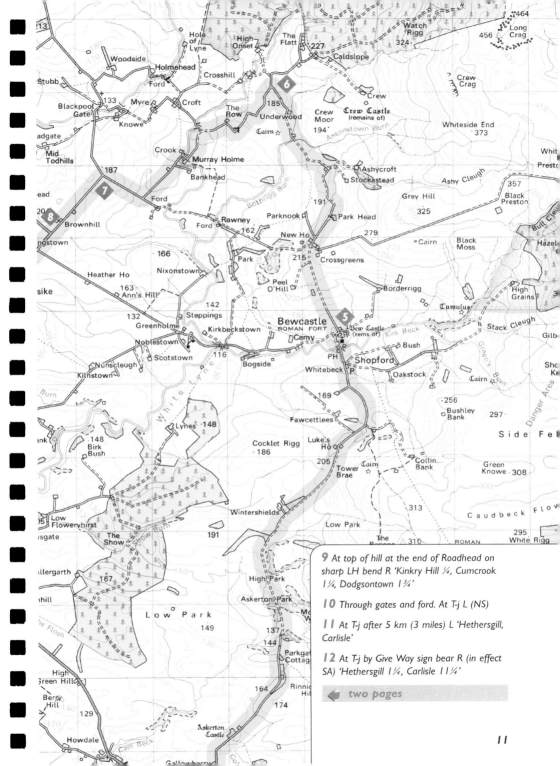

9 At top of hill at the end of Roadhead on sharp LH bend R 'Kinkry Hill ¼, Cumcrook 1¼, Dodgsontown 1¾'

10 Through gates and ford. At T-j L (NS)

11 At T-j after 5 km (3 miles) L 'Hethersgill, Carlisle'

12 At T-j by Give Way sign bear R (in effect SA) 'Hethersgill 1¼, Carlisle 11¼'

◀ **two pages**

11

South from Wetheral along the Eden Valley

Start

The Post Office, Wetheral

 No specific car park. Some space near to the Post Office

Distance and grade

45 km (28 miles) (or 26 km (16 miles) if the River Eden is crossed at Armathwaite)

 Easy / Moderate

Terrain

The valley of the River Eden is followed on its eastern side on the outward leg and on the western side on the return. However, the ride does not run along the banks of the river

The Eden Valley offers some of the finest cycling in Cumbria – it is relatively little-visited compared with the Lake District, there are fine views of both the Pennines and the Lakeland Fells, the hills are never too long or too steep and the River Eden itself is a constant delight. An option to shorten this ride to 26 km (16 miles) is suggested. The route makes use of the railway bridge over the Eden in Wetheral to cross to the eastern side of the river. There are alternating views of the Pennines and the river as you climb beyond Cumwhitton and then descend to the river near Holmwrangle. The steepest climb of the day is followed by a descent to the Nunnery House Hotel, a fine location for a coffee or tea stop. The river is crossed at Lazonby and is followed north through Armathwaite back to the start.

Wetheral

Cumwhitton

Holmwrangle

Armathwaite

Kirkos...

and there are three climbs: 115 m (380 ft) from Wetheral to Hornsby Gate, a steeper 106 m (350 ft) south from Armathwaite above Coombs Wood, and 85 m (280 ft) north from Lazonby back towards Armathwaite. Highest point – 161 m (530 ft) betwen Lazonby and Armathwaite. Lowest point – 39 m (130 ft) at the start

Nearest railway

Wetheral, Armathwaite or Lazonby

▲ *The Eden Valley*

Places of interest

Wetheral 1
Large stone houses stand around the triangular green, dominated by the 19th-century chateau-style Eden Bank

Corby Castle 2
The bulky 13th-century keep has 17th- and 19th-century additions. Terraced gardens overlook the River Eden with its medieval wood and stone salmon traps

Armathwaite 6
The village clusters around the bridge over the River Eden. The tower of the riverside castle was built into a Georgian mansion

Kirkoswald 7
Red-sandstone village with a 15th-century church and a ruined castle surrounded by a 13th-century moat. The college, the seat of the Featherstone family since 1613, was converted from a peel tower built in 1450

Refreshments

Wheatsheaf PH, Crown Hotel, **Wetheral**
Corby Bridge Inn PH, **Great Corby**
Pheasant Inn PH, **Cumwhitton**
Coffee and tea at Nunnery House Hotel, **Staffield**
Fetherston Arms PH, Crown Inn PH, **Kirkoswald**
Joiners Arms PH, Midland Hotel PH, **Lazonby**
Dukes Head PH ◆*, Fox and Pheasant PH,*
Armathwaite

Lazonby

Baronwood Park

Armathwaite

Knott Hill

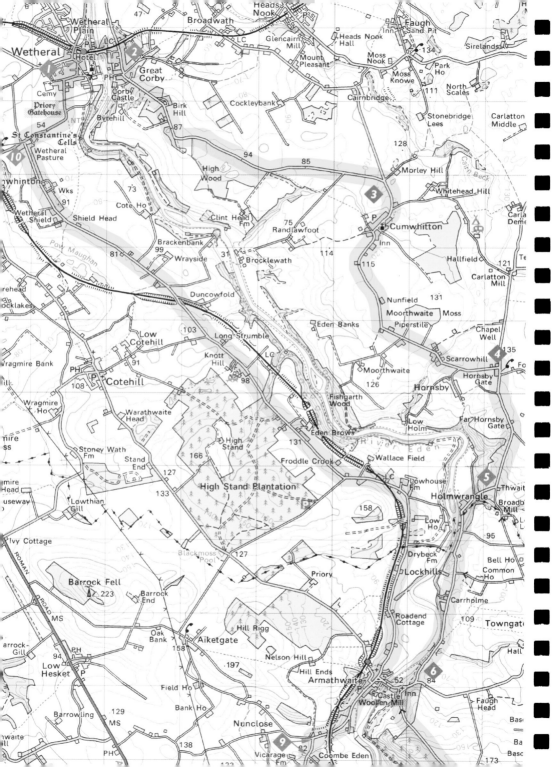

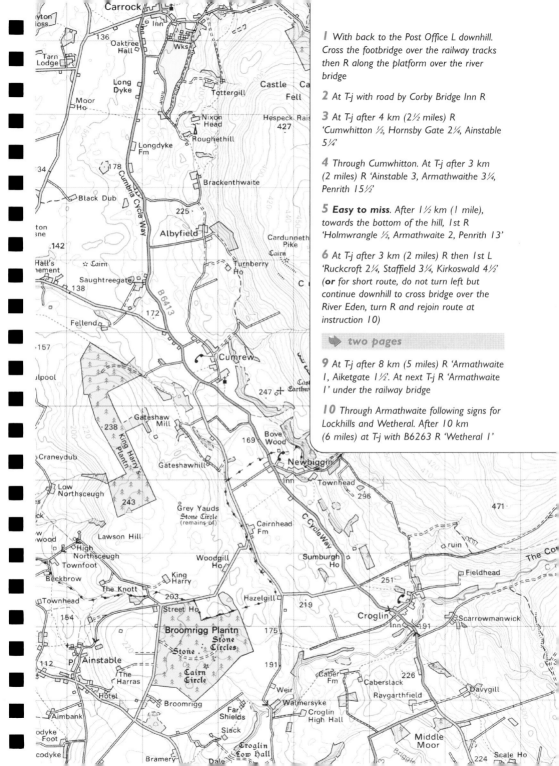

1 With back to the Post Office L downhill. Cross the footbridge over the railway tracks then R along the platform over the river bridge

2 At T-j with road by Corby Bridge Inn R

3 At T-j after 4 km (2½ miles) R 'Cumwhitton ½, Hornsby Gate 2¼, Ainstable 5¼

4 Through Cumwhitton. At T-j after 3 km (2 miles) R 'Ainstable 3, Armathwaithe 3¼, Penrith 15½'

5 **Easy to miss**. After 1½ km (1 mile), towards the bottom of the hill, 1st R 'Holmwrangle ½, Armathwaite 2, Penrith 13'

6 At T-j after 3 km (2 miles) R then 1st L 'Ruckcroft 2¼, Staffield 3¼, Kirkoswald 4½ (**or for short route, do not turn left but continue downhill to cross bridge over the River Eden, turn R and rejoin route at instruction 10**)

➡ **two pages**

9 At T-j after 8 km (5 miles) R 'Armathwaite 1, Aiketgate 1½'. At next T-j R 'Armathwaite 1' under the railway bridge

10 Through Armathwaite following signs for Lockhills and Wetheral. After 10 km (6 miles) at T-j with B6263 R 'Wetheral 1'

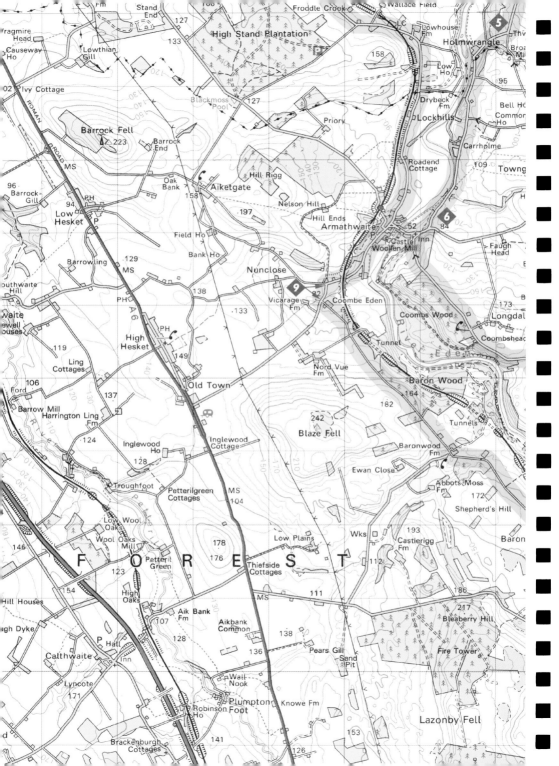

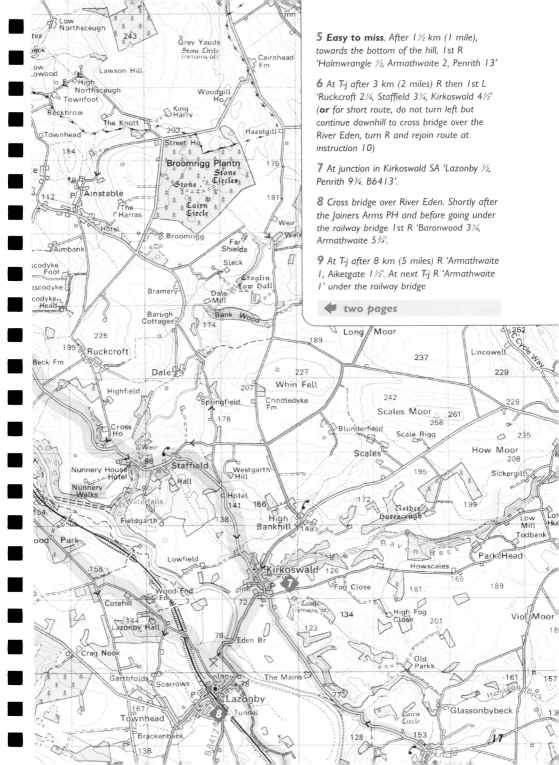

5 **Easy to miss**. After 1½ km (1 mile), towards the bottom of the hill, 1st R 'Holmwrangle ½, Armathwaite 2, Penrith 13'

6 At T-j after 3 km (2 miles) R then 1st L 'Ruckcroft 2¼, Staffield 3¼, Kirkoswald 4½' (**or** for short route, do not turn left but continue downhill to cross bridge over the River Eden, turn R and rejoin route at instruction 10)

7 At junction in Kirkoswald SA 'Lazonby ½, Penrith 9¾. B6413'.

8 Cross bridge over River Eden. Shortly after the Joiners Arms PH and before going under the railway bridge 1st R 'Baronwood 3¼, Armathwaite 5¾'.

9 At T-j after 8 km (5 miles) R 'Armathwaite 1, Aiketgate 1½'. At next T-j R 'Armathwaite 1' under the railway bridge

◀ two pages

North from Wigton to the coastline of the Solway Firth

3

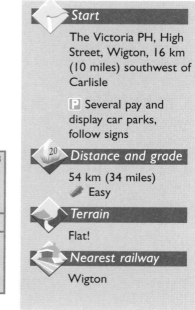

Start

The Victoria PH, High Street, Wigton, 16 km (10 miles) southwest of Carlisle

P Several pay and display car parks, follow signs

Distance and grade

54 km (34 miles)
Easy

Terrain

Flat!

Nearest railway

Wigton

It may come as a surprise to visitors to Cumbria that within the county boundaries there is an area that rivals East Anglia or the Somerset Levels for flatness! North of the A596, between Maryport on the

coast and Carlisle, there is a large expanse of countryside that rarely rises to above 30 m (100 feet). Although Wigton itself is not a place to linger, dominated as it is by its cellophane factory, you soon escape into the maze of quiet lanes across the levels of Wedholme Flow. This is one of those good conversational rides where it would be possible for long stretches to cycle side by side and put the world to right with little fear of being mown down by vehicles. The masts between Anthorn and Cadurnock act as a beacon for the first half of the ride. Expect to see many birds on the salt marshes near to Newton Arlosh. From the coast, you will be faced with clear views of Scotland across the Solway Firth, the fells to the south of Dumfries providing a pleasant contrast to the cooling towers of the power station at Annan. Soon after Port Carlisle, the coast is left behind as the ride cuts inland through a series of unusual sounding hamlets such as Whitrigglees, Wampool, Biglands and Drumleaning to return to Wigton.

Wigton   Waverbridge   Raby   Newton Arlosh   Whitrigg   Anthorn

Places of interest

Abbeytown *(just off the route)* 5
Monks founded Holme Cultram Abbey in
1150, grew grain, raised sheep and cattle
and traded in salt from the
estuary. At the Dissolution
of the Monasteries in the 16th
century, its stones were
hauled away to build houses

Refreshments

*Hare and Hounds PH 🍴, plenty of
choice in* **Wigton**
Bush Inn PH, **Angerton**
Kings Arms PH, **Bowness-on-Solway**
Hope and Anchor PH, **Port Carlisle**
Highland Laddie Inn PH, **Glasson**

Bowness-on-Solway 9
Roman soldiers guarded the
western end of Hadrian's Wall
here and a defensive ditch (vallum)
can be seen near Glasson. The wall
was built between AD122 and 139 to
discourage the independent Scottish tribes
from marauding into the largely pacified
territory to the south. It stretched 117 m
(73 miles) from Bowness to Wallsend-on-
Tyne. It was built of the materials most
readily at hand – stone in the east and turf
in the west

◀ *The Solway Firth
in February*

Bowness-on-Solway   Port Carlisle   Wampool   Biglands   Moorhouse

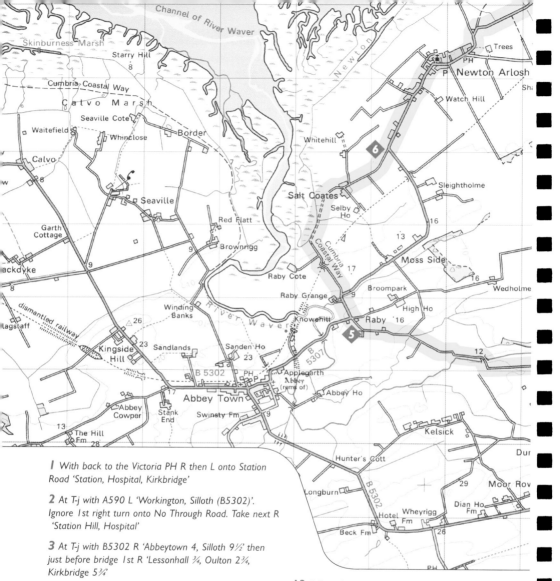

1 With back to the Victoria PH R then L onto Station Road 'Station, Hospital, Kirkbridge'

2 At T-j with A590 L 'Workington, Silloth (B5302)'. Ignore 1st right turn onto No Through Road. Take next R 'Station Hill, Hospital'

3 At T-j with B5302 R 'Abbeytown 4, Silloth 9½' then just before bridge 1st R 'Lessonhall ¾, Oulton 2¾, Kirkbridge 5¾'

4 After 1 km (¾ mile) 1st L in Lessonhall 'Newton Arlosh, Abbeytown'

5 At T-j with B5307 R 'Newton Arlosh 2½, Kirkbride 5'. (Join the Cumbria Cycleway at this point). 1st L on sharp RH bend 'Cumbria Cycleway'

6 At T-j with B5307 L 'Kirkbride 3, Carlisle 14'

➡ **two pages**

12 Follow this road for 8 km (5 miles) through various farms. At T-j R 'Moorhouse 1¼, Wigton 3'

13 **Easy to miss**. Ignore 1st left after 800 m (½ mile). Shortly after passing red sandstone terraced cottages to your right next L 'Wigton'

14 At T-j L 'Wigton 1'

15 At T-j with A596 R then L 'Wigton' to return to the start

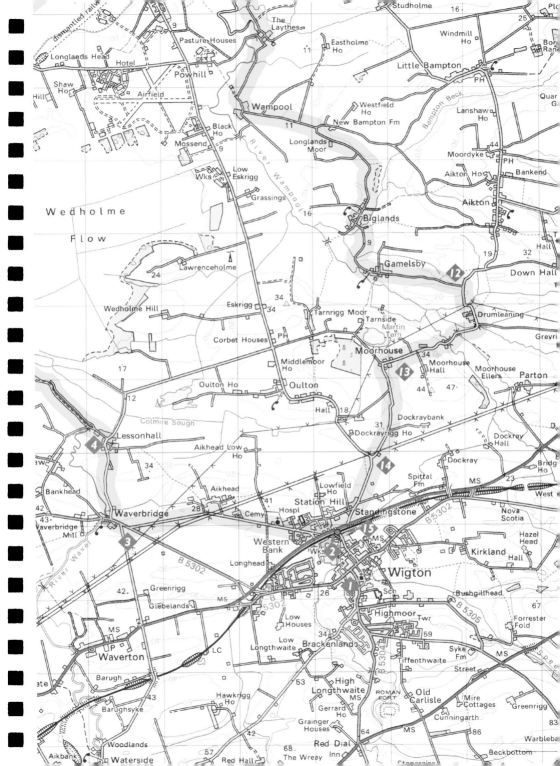

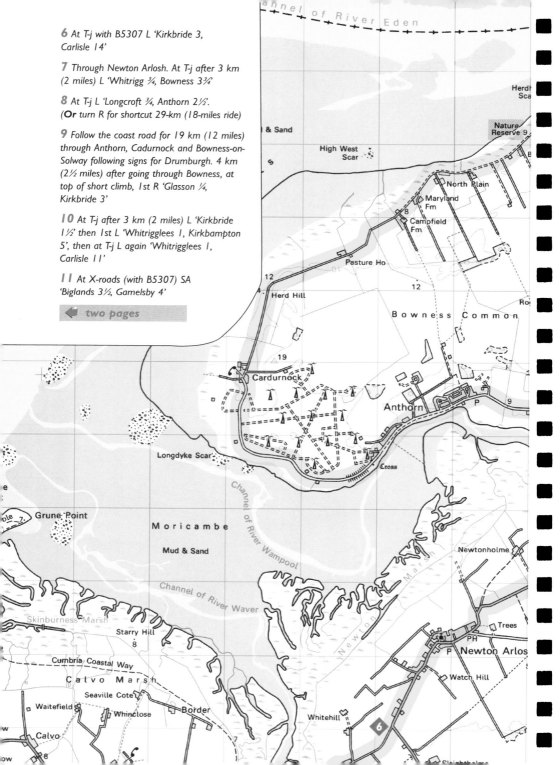

6 At T-j with B5307 L 'Kirkbride 3, Carlisle 14'

7 Through Newton Arlosh. At T-j after 3 km (2 miles) L 'Whitrigg ¾, Bowness 3¾'

8 At T-j L 'Longcroft ¾, Anthorn 2½'. (**Or** turn R for shortcut 29-km (18-miles ride)

9 Follow the coast road for 19 km (12 miles) through Anthorn, Cadurnock and Bowness-on-Solway following signs for Drumburgh. 4 km (2½ miles) after going through Bowness, at top of short climb, 1st R 'Glasson ¼, Kirkbride 3'

10 At T-j after 3 km (2 miles) L 'Kirkbride 1½' then 1st L 'Whitrigglees 1, Kirkbampton 5', then at T-j again 'Whitrigglees 1, Carlisle 11'

11 At X-roads (with B5307) SA 'Biglands 3½, Gamelsby 4'

◀ two pages

South from Cockermouth along the edge of the Lake District's Western Fells

 Start

Earl Mayo's statue,
High Street,
Cockermouth

🅿 Several pay and
display car parks

 Distance and grade

45 km (28 miles)
🢒🢒 Easy/moderate

 Terrain

For a ride with such
stupendous views,
there are few climbs to
worry about. Between
the crossing of the
River Marron in Ullock
up to the road beneath
Murton Fell, there is
183 m (600 ft) of
climbing – 70 m (230
ft) fairly steeply up to
Dean Cross, then 112
m (370 ft) more gently
from Asby to beyond
Kirkland. Highest point
– 259 m (850 ft)
beneath Murton Fell.
Lowest point – 45 m
(150 ft) at the start

 Nearest railway

Workington, 8 km
(5 miles) west of the
route at Greysouthen

This is a real gem of a ride with some reasonably good views of the fells. On the first half of the ride, you are slightly set back from the hills enabling yourself to appreciate them from afar. After Kirkland, the route

takes you into the heart of the hills. It is worth making a short detour from the T-junction beneath Murton Fell for some very fine views of Ennerdale Water with the backdrop of Ennerdale Fell. From Waterend, the views are dominated by the mass of Melbreak and the charms of Loweswater but if you are lucky and the visibility is good, you should be able to look right down the valley of Crummock Water and Buttermere to the very core of the central fells. There is an excellent pub in Loweswater, should you need a break before the quiet lane through Lorton Vale alongside the River Cocker takes you back into Cockermouth.

Cockermouth   Brigham   Greysouthen   Ullock   Asby   Kirkland

Places of interest

Cockermouth 1
William Wordsworth was born in a Georgian house at the end of the main street. There are the remains of a largely 14th-century castle at the junction of the Cocker and Derwent rivers

Refreshments

Brown Cow PH 🍺, plenty of choice in **Cockermouth**
Royal Yew PH 🍺, **Dean**
Coffee and tea at the Grange Country House Hotel **at the northern end of Loweswater**
Kirkstile Inn PH 🍺 🍺, **Loweswater**

The Lortons 16
Lorton Hall is partly a 15th-century peel tower, built as a refuge for the villagers against raiding Scots during the Border wars. The Jennings brewery in Cockermouth started off in what is now the village hall in High Lorton. At the rear stands a yew tree under which the founder of the Quaker movement, George Fox, preached pacifism to a large crowd that included Cromwellian soldiers. William Wordsworth in his poem Yew Trees wrote:

'There is a yew tree, pride of Lorton Vale
Which to this day stands single, in the midst
Of its own darkness, as it stood of yore'

▼ *Crummock Water*

Felldyke   Lamplugh   Waterend   Loweswater   Thackthwaite   Low Lorton

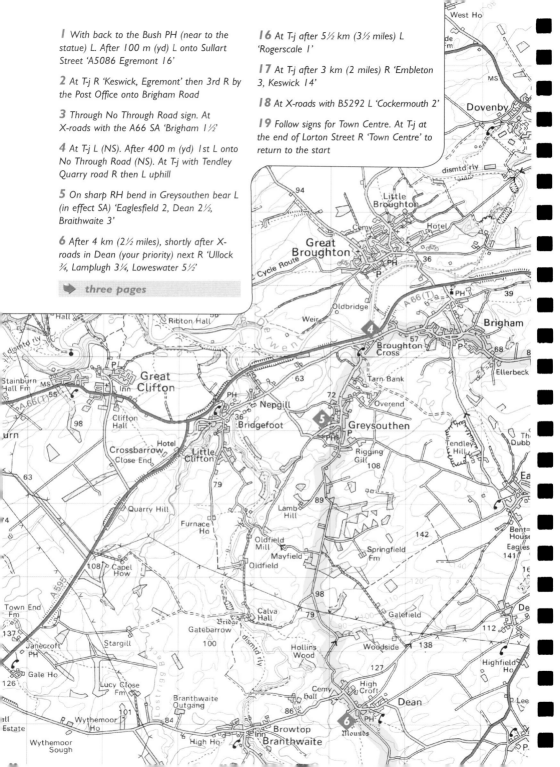

1 With back to the Bush PH (near to the statue) L. After 100 m (yd) L onto Sullart Street 'A5086 Egremont 16'

2 At T-j R 'Keswick, Egremont' then 3rd R by the Post Office onto Brigham Road

3 Through No Through Road sign. At X-roads with the A66 SA 'Brigham 1½'

4 At T-j L (NS). After 400 m (yd) 1st L onto No Through Road (NS). At T-j with Tendley Quarry road R then L uphill

5 On sharp RH bend in Greysouthen bear L (in effect SA) 'Eaglesfield 2, Dean 2½, Braithwaite 3'

6 After 4 km (2½ miles), shortly after X-roads in Dean (your priority) next R 'Ullock ¾, Lamplugh 3¼, Loweswater 5½'

➡ *three pages*

16 At T-j after 5½ km (3½ miles) L 'Rogerscale 1'

17 At T-j after 3 km (2 miles) R 'Embleton 3, Keswick 14'

18 At X-roads with B5292 L 'Cockermouth 2'

19 Follow signs for Town Centre. At T-j at the end of Lorton Street R 'Town Centre' to return to the start

Take care not to mistake the faded yellow line of the national park boundary for the solid yellow line of the route

27

Take care not to mistake the faded yellow line of the national park boundary for the solid yellow line of the route

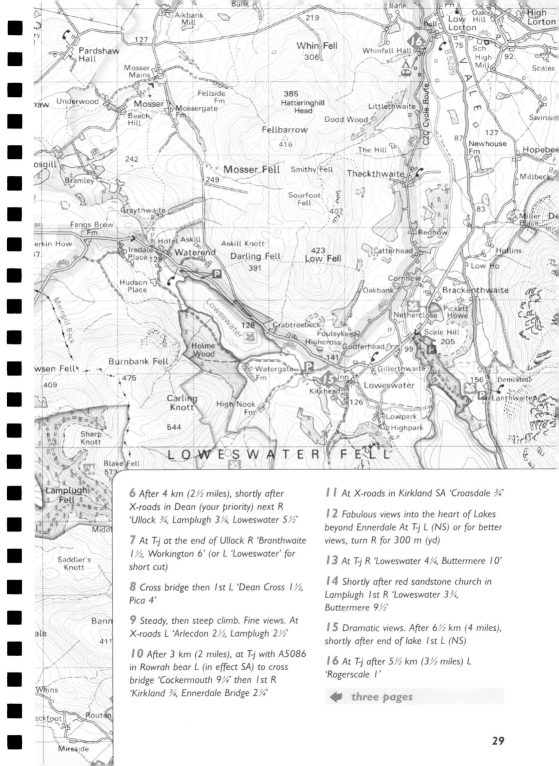

6 After 4 km (2½ miles), shortly after X-roads in Dean (your priority) next R 'Ullock ¾, Lamplugh 3¼, Loweswater 5½'

7 At T-j at the end of Ullock R 'Branthwaite 1½, Workington 6' (or L 'Loweswater' for short cut)

8 Cross bridge then 1st L 'Dean Cross 1½, Pica 4'

9 Steady, then steep climb. Fine views. At X-roads L 'Arlecdon 2½, Lamplugh 2½'

10 After 3 km (2 miles), at T-j with A5086 in Rowrah bear L (in effect SA) to cross bridge 'Cockermouth 9¼' then 1st R 'Kirkland ¾, Ennerdale Bridge 2¼'

11 At X-roads in Kirkland SA 'Croasdale ¾'

12 Fabulous views into the heart of Lakes beyond Ennerdale At T-j L (NS) or for better views, turn R for 300 m (yd)

13 At T-j R 'Loweswater 4¼, Buttermere 10'

14 Shortly after red sandstone church in Lamplugh 1st R 'Loweswater 3¾, Buttermere 9½'

15 Dramatic views. After 6½ km (4 miles), shortly after end of lake 1st L (NS)

16 At T-j after 5½ km (3½ miles) L 'Rogerscale 1'

◀ **three pages**

5 A tour around Skiddaw and Blencathra, north from Keswick

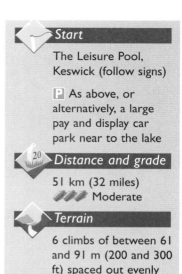

Start

The Leisure Pool, Keswick (follow signs)

P As above, or alternatively, a large pay and display car park near to the lake

Distance and grade

51 km (32 miles)
/// Moderate

Terrain

6 climbs of between 61 and 91 m (200 and 300 ft) spaced out evenly through the ride. The least welcome is that at the end from the main road up to

Skiddaw and Blencathra are completely circumnavigated on this ride, almost entirely on quiet lanes. The contrast between the described exit from Keswick, along the railway path, and the parallel A66 could not be greater. One is a delightful woodland trail crossing the River Greta some seven times on a gently graded trail popular with walkers and cyclists alike. By contrast, the A66 is a fast, noisy, busy trunk road that holds no appeal whatsoever to cyclists. By using a section of old road at the end of Threlkeld, it is possible to minimise to a couple of 100 m (yd) the time spent on the A66. The views of Blencathra from the tiny lanes in the valley by Guardhouse are truly wonderful. The fell road from the White Horse Inn at Scales climbs then contours around the flanks of Souther Fell. There is a choice of refreshments at the inn at Mungrisdale or the coffee shop at Mosedale, or perhaps you will wish to cross the corner of the Caldbeck Fells before dropping down to Hesket Newmarket, which is at the halfway stage of the ride. The views towards Skiddaw improve as you climb to a high point on Aughertree Fell. The short section on the A591 after Bassenthwaite and Scarness comes as something of a shock after so long on quiet roads but the first available exit is taken up to Applethwaite. All along this stretch, the views across to Grisedale Pike and the fells above Bassenthwaite Lake are magnificent.

Keswick   Threlkeld   Scales   Mungrisdale   Mosedale

Applethwaite, but if the visibility is good, then the views of the fells on the other side of the valley are more than adequate compensation. Highest point – 314 m (1030 ft) at Calebreck, south of Hesket Newmarket. Lowest point – 85 m (280 ft) at the start

Nearest railway

Penrith

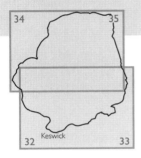

Places of interest

Keswick 1
Several museums with a variety of displays, including lead pencils made here since the 16th-century, originally with local graphite, a relief model of the Lake District, works by Lakeland poets and cars used in films and TV series. Coleridge and Southey lived here

Castlerigg Stone Circle 1
A Bronze Age ring of stones up to 1 m (6 ft) tall set in an amphitheatre of hills. Probably 3500 years old

Threlkeld 2
Famous for fox-hunting and sheepdog trials. Stagecoach travellers used to stay at the 17th-century Horse and Farrier Inn

Bassenthwaite 14
There are traces of Roman and Norse settlements around the village

Refreshments

Plenty of choice in **Keswick**
Horse and Farrier PH, Salutation Inn PH 🍴,
Threlkeld White Horse Inn PH, **Scales**
Mill Inn PH 🍴, **Mungrisdale**
Quakers coffee and tea shop at **Mosedale**
Old Crown PH 🍴🍴, **Hesket Newmarket**
Sun Inn PH 🍴🍴, **Bassenthwaite**

Aughertree   Longlands   Orthwaite   Bassenthwaite   Millbeck

1 From the leisure pool, follow the broad track (the old railway track) past the old station through several gates and over many bridges to its end

2 Follow signs for Threlkeld village. At the A66 L and L again 'Threlkeld ¼'

3 Through Threlkeld past the Horse and Farrier PH and the Salutation Inn. 100 m (yd) before rejoining the A66 L onto No Through Road just past the telephone box on the left

4 Through gates to the end of the tarmac. Descend on path to the A66. Turn L then 1st R 'Guardhouse'

5 At T-j after 1½ km (1 mile), with No Through Road to the right, turn L

6 At T-j by triangle of grass and Give Way sign L. At T-j with A66 L then R 'White Horse Inn'. Just before Inn sharp R back on yourself 'Gates'

7 After 5 km (3 miles) at T-j just past Mill Inn L (NS)

➡ **three pages**

17 At T-j with A591 R 'Keswick'

18 After 4 km (2½ miles) 1st L 'Millbeck, Applethwaite, Skiddaw'

19 At T-j after 4 km (2½ miles) L. At roundabout SA onto A5771 'Keswick'

20 1st L after the Pheasant Inn onto Brundholme Road 'Railway Station, Leisure Pool'

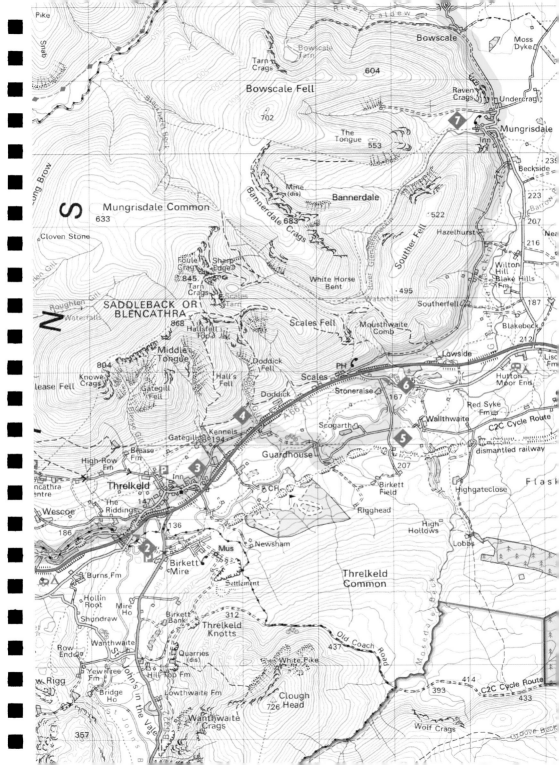

Take care not to mistake the faded yellow line of the national park boundary for the solid yellow line of the route

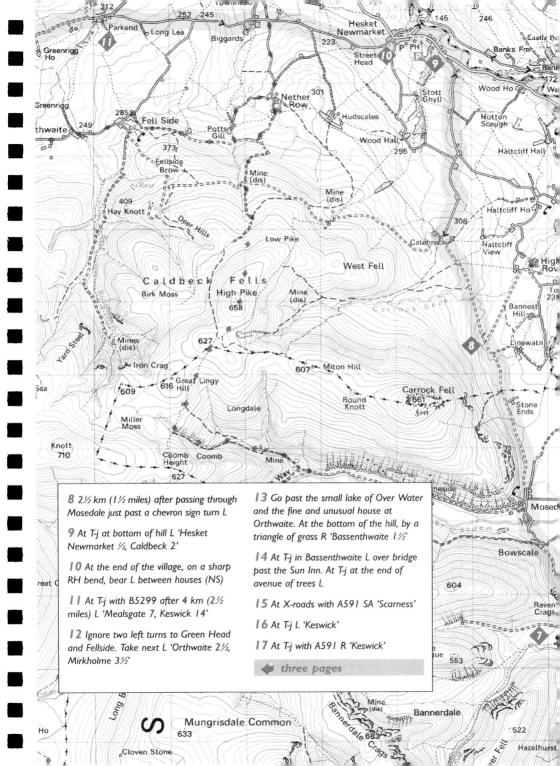

8 2½ km (1½ miles) after passing through Mosedale just past a chevron sign turn L

9 At T-j at bottom of hill L 'Hesket Newmarket ½, Caldbeck 2'

10 At the end of the village, on a sharp RH bend, bear L between houses (NS)

11 At T-j with B5299 after 4 km (2½ miles) L 'Mealsgate 7, Keswick 14'

12 Ignore two left turns to Green Head and Fellside. Take next L 'Orthwaite 2½, Mirkholme 3½'

13 Go past the small lake of Over Water and the fine and unusual house at Orthwaite. At the bottom of the hill, by a triangle of grass R 'Bassenthwaite 1½'

14 At T-j in Bassenthwaite L over bridge past the Sun Inn. At T-j at the end of avenue of trees L

15 At X-roads with A591 SA 'Scarness'

16 At T-j L 'Keswick'

17 At T-j with A591 R 'Keswick'

◀ *three pages*

Along the Eden Valley northwest from Appleby

Start

Tourist Information Centre, Appleby-in-Westmorland

🅿 Long-stay car park near the swimming pool at the end of Chapel Street. From the Tourist Information Centre turn R uphill then 1st R onto High Wiend and R again along Chapel Street

*T*he Eden Valley is a real delight for cyclists: to the east, lie the Pennines, away to the west, loom the fells of the Lake District, between the two, runs the River Eden with long stretches of relatively easy cycling with fabulous views of both

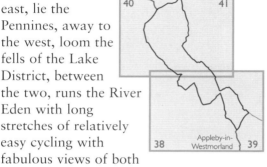

mountain ranges. This ride runs in a cigar-shaped loop northwest from Appleby through countryside, which is more fertile and thus more cultivated than the surrounding fells. There are signs of red sandstone in the houses and the dry-stone walls enclosing rolling green pastures as you pass through solid, handsome villages and hamlets at the base of the western edge of the Pennines.

Distance and grade

59 km (37 miles)

🚴🚴 Easy / moderate

Terrain

Undulating. Several climbs of between 30 and 61 m (100 and 200 ft). 9 m (30 ft) climb west from Little Salkeld. Highest point – 216 m (710 ft) at Knock, north of Dufton. Lowest point – 91 m (300 ft) at Little Salkeld

Nearest railway

Appleby-in-Westmorland

Appleby-in-Westmorland · Long Marton · Kirkby Thore · Newbiggin · Culgaith · Langwathby · Little Salkeld

Appleby-in-Westmorland 1

The former capital of Westmorland, consisting of two towns either side of the River Eden. The old town was a

▼ *Long Meg, near Little Salked*

10th-century Danish village on a bluff overlooking the 'new' town that grew around the 12th-century castle. The latter was restored in the 1650s and has the original keep and a rare breeds farm. The town contains many splendid buildings from the Jacobean to Victorian times. The town is famous for its lively and colourful horse fair, held every June, when gypsy horse-dealers from all over the country come to the town for horse racing and trading

Milburn 3

Attractive village lying in the shadows of 893 m (2930 ft) Cross Fell, which rises up behind the sandstone cottages huddled around the spacious green. All face inwards, a reminder of the days when bands of bloodthirsty outlaws roamed the wild borderland between England and Scotland, killing, burning and rustling sheep and cattle. The narrow entrances at each corner were easily sealed against border raiders. A lofty maypole, topped by a weathercock, stands on the base of a long-gone preaching cross

Refreshments

Royal Oak PH 🍷 🍷, *plenty of choice in* **Appleby-in-Westmorland**
Masons Arms PH, **Long Marton**
Shepherds Inn PH 🍷, **Langwathby**
Post Haste Cafe, Shepherds Inn PH 🍷 🍷,
Melmerby *Fox Inn PH,* **Ousby**
Sun Inn PH, **Skirwith**
Stag Inn PH, **Milburn**
Stag Inn PH, **Dufton**

Great Salkeld *(just off the route)* 7

Red sandstone cottages and farmhouses cluster around the part-Norman church of St Cuthbert, which has a Norman dog-tooth carving on the south doorway. The ivy-clad tower was built in 1380 as a refuge for villagers against border raiders

Gamblesby Melmerby Ousby Blencarn Milburn Knock Dufton

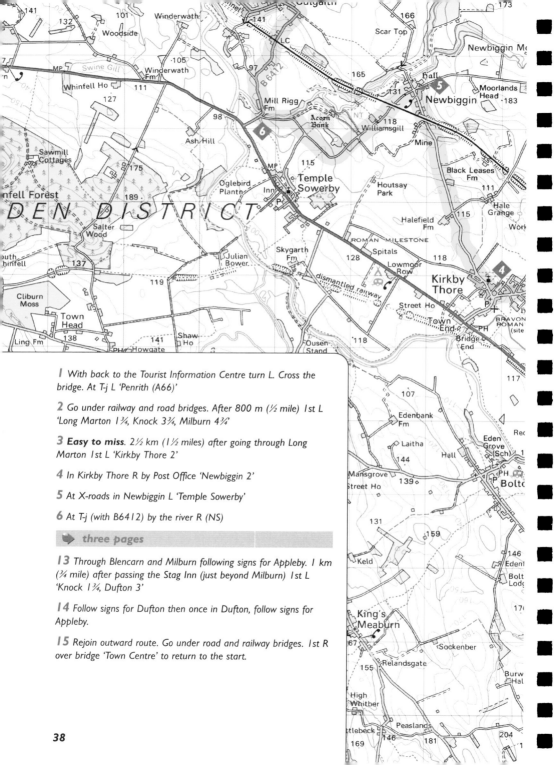

1 With back to the Tourist Information Centre turn L. Cross the bridge. At T-j L 'Penrith (A66)'

2 Go under railway and road bridges. After 800 m (½ mile) 1st L 'Long Marton 1¾, Knock 3¾, Milburn 4¾'

3 Easy to miss. 2½ km (1½ miles) after going through Long Marton 1st L 'Kirkby Thore 2'

4 In Kirkby Thore R by Post Office 'Newbiggin 2'

5 At X-roads in Newbiggin L 'Temple Sowerby'

6 At T-j (with B6412) by the river R (NS)

➡ **three pages**

13 Through Blencarn and Milburn following signs for Appleby. 1 km (¾ mile) after passing the Stag Inn (just beyond Milburn) 1st L 'Knock 1¾, Dufton 3'

14 Follow signs for Dufton then once in Dufton, follow signs for Appleby.

15 Rejoin outward route. Go under road and railway bridges. 1st R over bridge 'Town Centre' to return to the start.

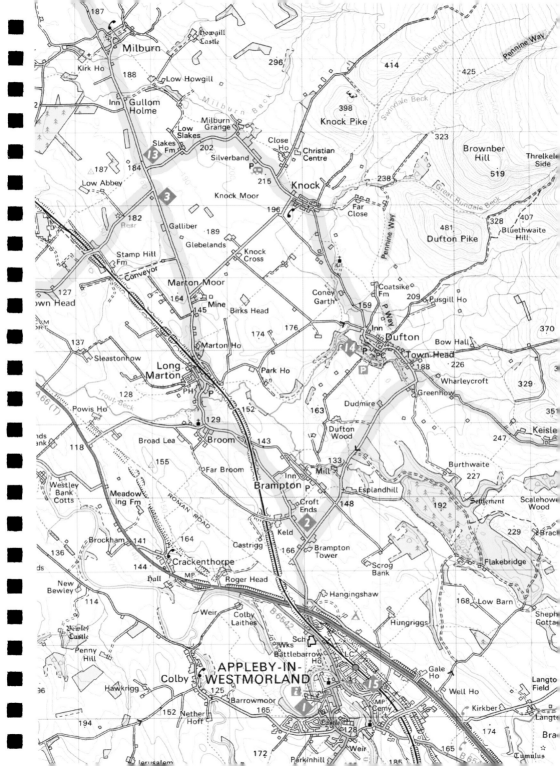

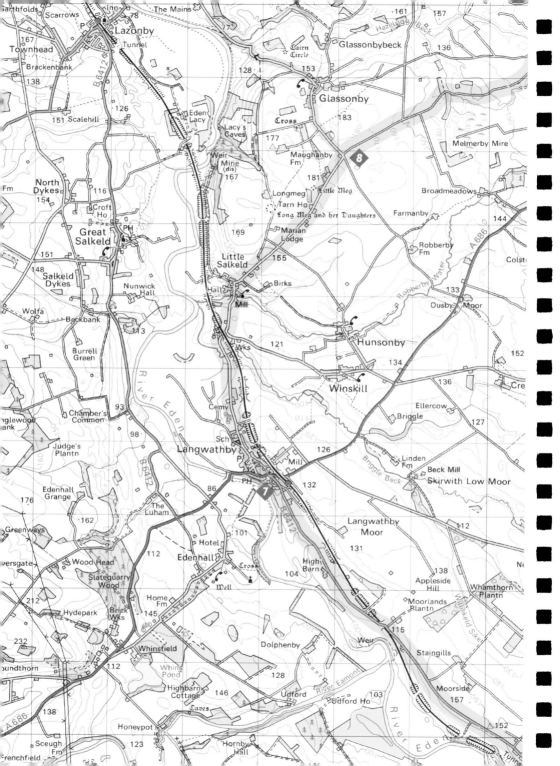

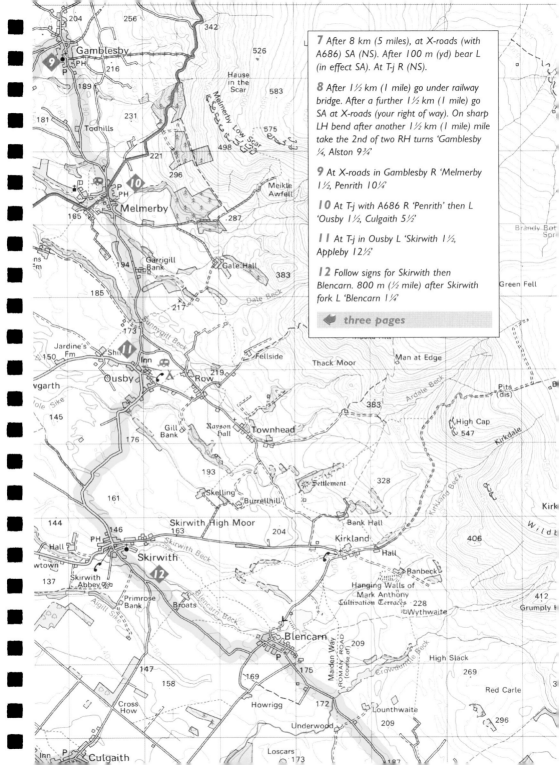

7 *After 8 km (5 miles), at X-roads (with A686) SA (NS). After 100 m (yd) bear L (in effect SA). At T-j R (NS).*

8 *After 1½ km (1 mile) go under railway bridge. After a further 1½ km (1 mile) go SA at X-roads (your right of way). On sharp LH bend after another 1½ km (1 mile) mile take the 2nd of two RH turns 'Gamblesby ¼, Alston 9¾'*

9 *At X-roads in Gamblesby R 'Melmerby 1½, Penrith 10¼'*

10 *At T-j with A686 R 'Penrith' then L 'Ousby 1½, Culgaith 5½'*

11 *At T-j in Ousby L 'Skirwith 1½, Appleby 12½'*

12 *Follow signs for Skirwith then Blencarn. 800 m (½ mile) after Skirwith fork L 'Blencarn 1¼'*

◀ **three pages**

West from Appleby to Shap and Askham, beneath the Lakeland Fells

*T*he first half of this ride is characterised by climbs in and out of river valleys:

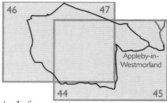

the River Eden is left behind at Appleby before a swift up and down to one of its tributaries, Hoff Beck at Colby. This in turn is crossed as the route heads east up over the hills and down into the valley of the River Lyvennet. There is a respite from the climbing as the valley is followed to Crosby Ravensworh with its lovely church and ring of prehistoric settlements. The steepest challenge of the day takes you up to over 300 m (1000 ft) with fabulous views across to the Lakeland fells. After Shap, you descend to the last important river valley – which formed by the River Lowther, drains the Haweswater Reservoir and borders Lowther Park with its dramatic castle facade. The last section of the ride seems to encourage you to stretch your legs and aim straight as an arrow for the gastronomic delights of Appleby.

 Start

Tourist Information Centre, Appleby-in-Westmorland

P Long-stay car park near the swimming pool at the end of Chapel Street. From the Tourist Information Centre turn R uphill then 1st R onto High Wiend and R again along Chapel Street

 Distance and grade

54 km (34 miles)
Moderate

 Terrain

Three climbs: 76 m (250 ft) west from Colby, 143 m (470 ft) west from Crosby Ravensworth, with the first section very steep, 70 m (230 ft) inside Lowther Park. Highest point – 329 m (1080 ft) above Crosby Ravensworth. Lowest point – 115 m (380 ft) at the end of the ride just before Appleby

 Nearest railway

Appleby-in-Westmorland

Appleby-in-Westmorland   Colby   King's Meaburn   Maulds Meaburn   Crosby Ravensworth   Shap

Crosby Ravensworth 6

The prehistoric settlements comprise many ruined huts, one measuring 15 m (50 ft) across. St Lawrence's Church is a cathedral in miniature, much rebuilt since the 13th-century and located in a picturesque setting

▼ *Near Shap*

Askham 11

An immaculate village on the steep wooded bank of the River Lowther. The upper green has fine views to Lowther Castle and the Pennines. There is an ancient stone circle and burial sites on Askham Fell

Lowther 12

The fairy-tale facade of towers, turrets and battlements is the only remnant of the 19th-century castle that was demolished in 1957. Lowther Park was created in 1283 for the estate's deer and is now a country park with nature trails, children's entertainments, rare breeds and red deer whose ancestors roamed the original deer park

Refreshments

Royal Oak PH ❦ ❦, *plenty of choice in*
Appleby-in-Westmorland
Butchers Arms PH ❦, **Crosby Ravensworth**
Cafe, Bulls Head PH ❦, **Shap**
Crown and Mitre PH, St Patricks Well PH ❦,
Bampton *(just off the route)*
Punchbowl PH ❦ ❦, *Queens Head PH* ❦,
Askham

Whale   Askham   Cliburn   Bolton   Colby

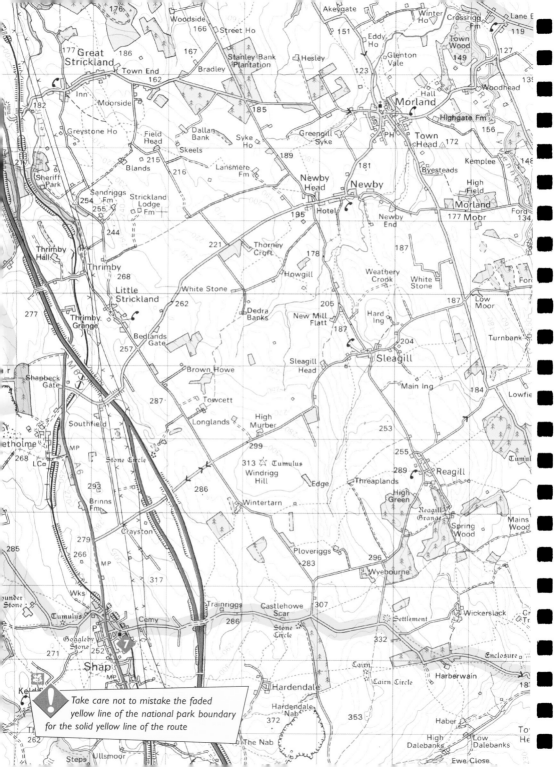

Take care not to mistake the faded
yellow line of the national park boundary
for the solid yellow line of the route

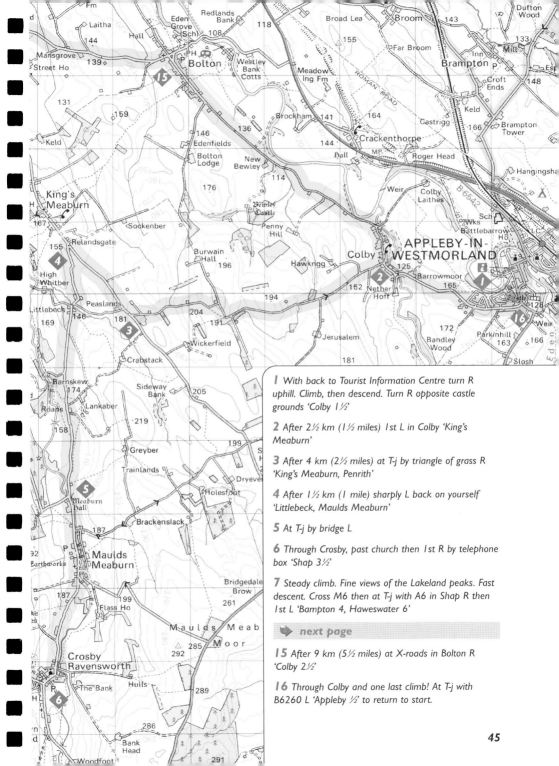

1 With back to Tourist Information Centre turn R uphill. Climb, then descend. Turn R opposite castle grounds 'Colby 1½'

2 After 2½ km (1½ miles) 1st L in Colby 'King's Meaburn'

3 After 4 km (2½ miles) at T-j by triangle of grass R 'King's Meaburn, Penrith'

4 After 1½ km (1 mile) sharply L back on yourself 'Littlebeck, Maulds Meaburn'

5 At T-j by bridge L

6 Through Crosby, past church then 1st R by telephone box 'Shap 3½'

7 Steady climb. Fine views of the Lakeland peaks. Fast descent. Cross M6 then at T-j with A6 in Shap R then 1st L 'Bampton 4, Haweswater 6'

➧ *next page*

15 After 9 km (5½ miles) at X-roads in Bolton R 'Colby 2½'

16 Through Colby and one last climb! At T-j with B6260 L 'Appleby ½' to return to start.

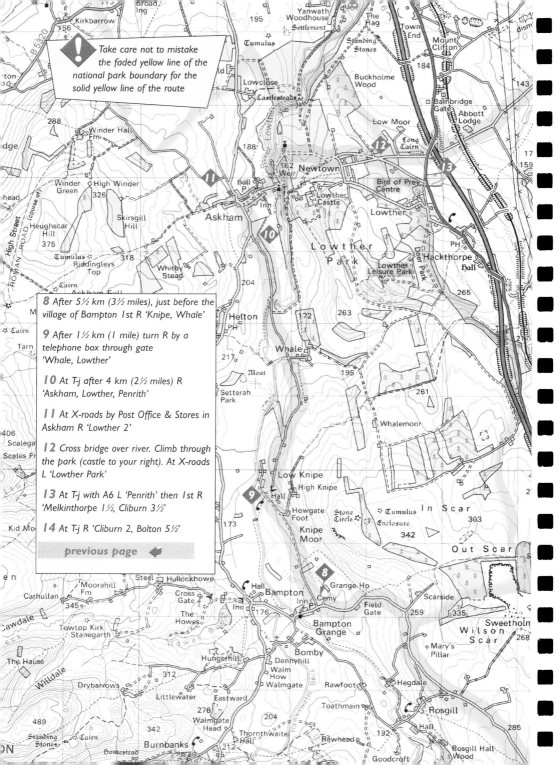

> ⚠ Take care not to mistake the faded yellow line of the national park boundary for the solid yellow line of the route

8 After 5½ km (3½ miles), just before the village of Bampton 1st R 'Knipe, Whale'

9 After 1½ km (1 mile) turn R by a telephone box through gate 'Whale, Lowther'

10 At T-j after 4 km (2½ miles) R 'Askham, Lowther, Penrith'

11 At X-roads by Post Office & Stores in Askham R 'Lowther 2'

12 Cross bridge over river. Climb through the park (castle to your right). At X-roads L 'Lowther Park'

13 At T-j with A6 L 'Penrith' then 1st R 'Melkinthorpe 1½, Cliburn 3½'

14 At T-j R 'Cliburn 2, Bolton 5½'

previous page ⬅

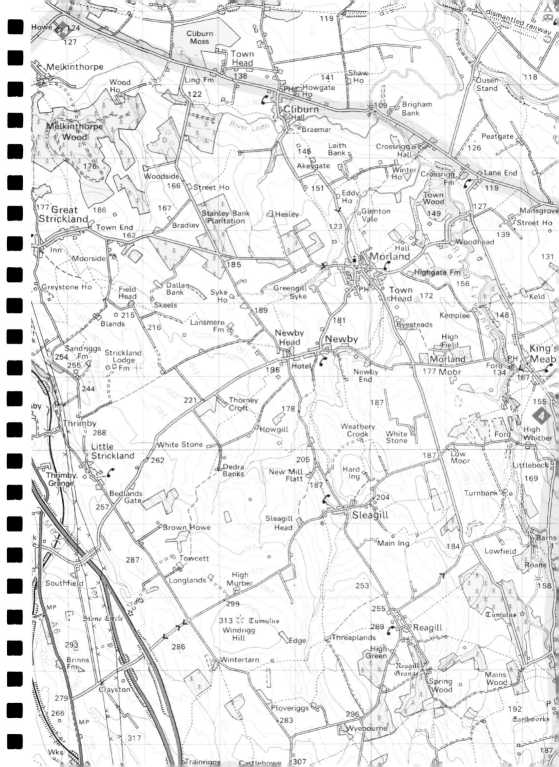

Southeast from Appleby-in-Westmorland to Brough and Kirkby Stephen

*T*his ride climbs out of the Eden valley, leaving behind the river, the railway and the main road (the A66) as it heads for quiet lanes running right along the base of the Pennines. The latter rise to over 610 m

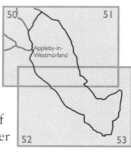

(2000 ft) within a couple of miles of the route. The ride passes through military firing ranges during the first section of the route before crossing to the south of the A66 and into Brough. There used to be seventeen inns here in its heyday as a staging post. The number has declined but you should find enough choice of cafés or pubs before turning south on a 4 km (2½ mile) section of main road. You are soon back onto quiet lanes through Winton and the charms of Kirkby Stephen. The 14 km (9 mile) final stretch back to Appleby is truly wonderful cycling – a gently undulating road with fine views to both sides and little traffic.

 Start

Tourist Information Centre, Appleby-in-Westmorland

🅿 Long-stay car park near the swimming pool at the end of Chapel Street. From the Tourist Information Centre turn R uphill then 1st R onto High Wiend and R again along Chapel Street

 Distance and grade

48 km (30 miles)
🔷🔷 Easy/moderate

Terrain

137 m (450 ft) climb near the start from the crossing of Trout Beck north of Appleby towards Murton. Several climbs of between 30 and 61 m (100 and 200 ft). Highest point – 271 m (890 ft) north of Murton. Lowest point – Appleby 125 m (410 ft)

 Nearest railway

Appleby-in-Westmorland

Appleby-in-Westmorland · Dufton · Murton · Hilton · Warcop · Great Musgrave

Brough 8

The castle was built by the Normans on the site of a Roman fort, then rebuilt in medieval style but was gutted by fire in 1666. Castle Hotel has original stables and outbuildings and a

▼ Brough Castle

cobbled courtyard. Stone from the Roman fort was used in building the 11th-century St Michael's Church. Great prosperity came in the 18th and 19th-centuries, with up to 60 stagecoaches a day halting at the village, on their way from London to Carlisle and on to Glasgow, or from York to Lancaster. Seventeen inns attended to their needs, but decline set in when the railway was built and routed to the west, through Kirkby Stephen

Kirkby Stephen 12

Brightly painted shops and old coaching inns huddle among attractive cobbled squares above the Eden valley. Inside the 13th-century St Stephen's church is the shaft of the unique 10th-century cemetery cross of Loki, the Danish Devil

Refreshments

Royal Oak PH ❦ ❦, plenty of choice in **Appleby-in-Westmorland**
Chamley Arms PH, **Warcop**
Plenty of choice in **Brough**
Bay Horse Inn PH, **Winton**
Kings Arms PH ❦, White Lion PH ❦, **Kirkby Stephen**

Winton   Kirkby Stephen   Soulby

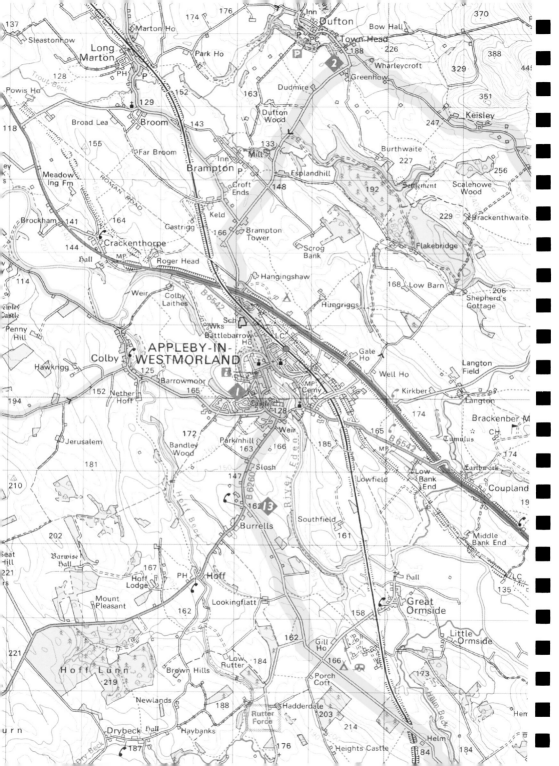

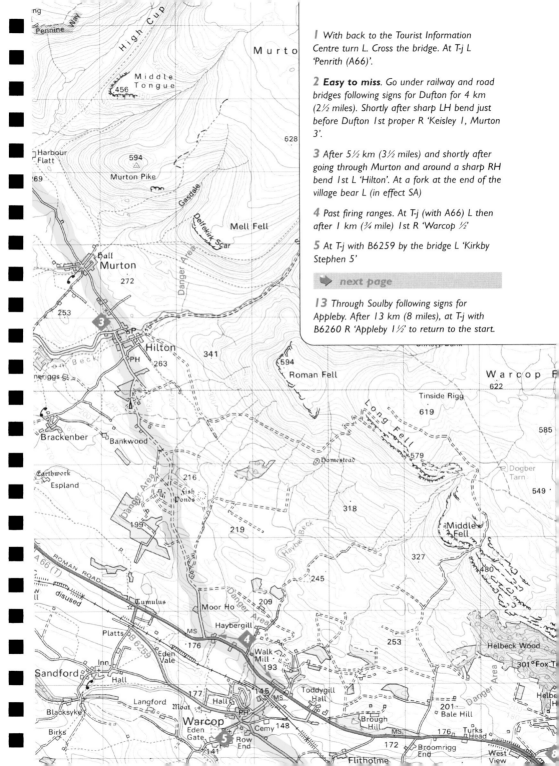

1 With back to the Tourist Information Centre turn L. Cross the bridge. At T-j L 'Penrith (A66)'.

2 Easy to miss. Go under railway and road bridges following signs for Dufton for 4 km (2½ miles). Shortly after sharp LH bend just before Dufton 1st proper R 'Keisley 1, Murton 3'.

3 After 5½ km (3½ miles) and shortly after going through Murton and around a sharp RH bend 1st L 'Hilton'. At a fork at the end of the village bear L (in effect SA)

4 Past firing ranges. At T-j (with A66) L then after 1 km (¾ mile) 1st R 'Warcop ½'

5 At T-j with B6259 by the bridge L 'Kirkby Stephen 5'

⮞ next page

13 Through Soulby following signs for Appleby. After 13 km (8 miles), at T-j with B6260 R 'Appleby 1½' to return to the start.

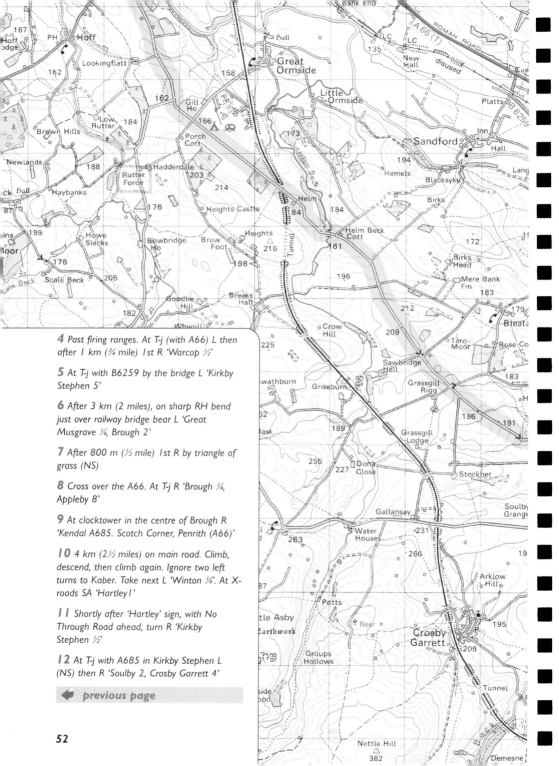

4 Past firing ranges. At T-j (with A66) L then after 1 km (¾ mile) 1st R 'Warcop ½'

5 At T-j with B6259 by the bridge L 'Kirkby Stephen 5'

6 After 3 km (2 miles), on sharp RH bend just over railway bridge bear L 'Great Musgrave ¼, Brough 2'

7 After 800 m (½ mile) 1st R by triangle of grass (NS)

8 Cross over the A66. At T-j R 'Brough ¼, Appleby 8'

9 At clocktower in the centre of Brough R 'Kendal A685. Scotch Corner, Penrith (A66)'

10 4 km (2½ miles) on main road. Climb, descend, then climb again. Ignore two left turns to Kaber. Take next L 'Winton ¼'. At X-roads SA 'Hartley1'

11 Shortly after 'Hartley' sign, with No Through Road ahead, turn R 'Kirkby Stephen ½'

12 At T-j with A685 in Kirkby Stephen L (NS) then R 'Soulby 2, Crosby Garrett 4'

◀ previous page

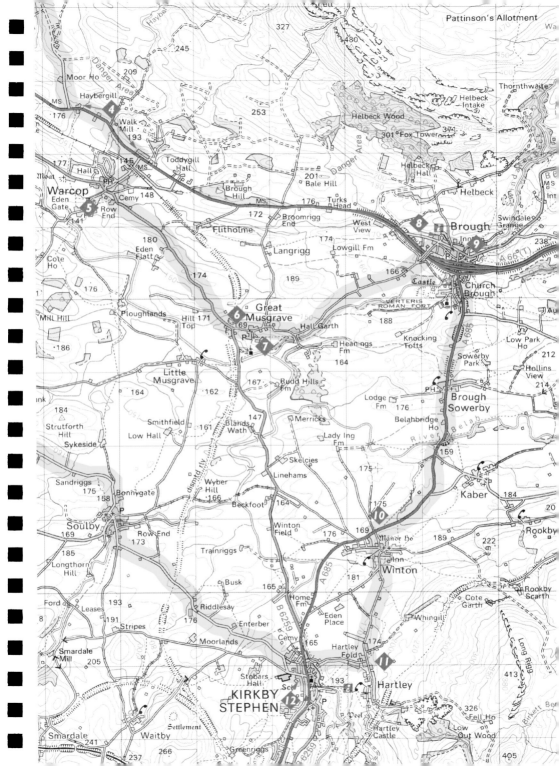

North from Kendal along quiet lanes into the valleys of the Mint, Sprint and Dent

Start

The Tourist Information Centre, Kendal

🅿 Follow signs for long-stay car parks

Distance and grade

53½ km (33½ miles)

🚲🚲🚲 Moderate / strenuous

Terrain

186 m (610 ft) climb from the start to the edge of Hay Fell. 131 m (430 ft) climb south from Staveley. 146 m (480 ft) near the start of Underbarrow up over Scout Scar. Many

Although Kendal itself is dominated by motor traffic, within 1.5 km (1 mile) or so of the town centre, it is possible to escape onto quiet lanes with some of the most rewarding cycling in the Lake District. The price to be paid for this is a steep climb of over 180 m (600 ft) on the old Sedbergh road to the edge of Hay Fell. From here

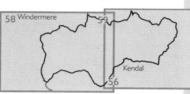

on, the route is truly delightful with tiny hamlets, fine views, streams and sections of broadleaf woodland. Staveley is the only village of any size in the first half of the ride. From Staveley, tiny, gated roads lead west, then south through Borwick Fold. The route continues on to Winster and towards Bowland Bridge where there are two excellent pubs just off the route. You are faced with a last climb over the southern end of Scout Scar to return to Kendal, the road dropping you right at the doorstep of the Tourist Information Centre. (The obvious direct route over Scout Scar is a steeper climb on a busier road, hence the southern route).

Kendal   Woodside   Beck Houses   Grayrigg   Patton Bridge   Garnett Bridge   Staveley

of the black arrows in the middle section of the ride are for very short sections and should cause no worries. Highest point – 231 m (760 ft) near the start, to the east of Kendal. Lowest point – 9 m (30 ft) at Underbarrow

Nearest railway

Kendal

Places of interest

Kendal 1

Isolated above the 'auld grey town' of fine limestone buildings and narrow twisting streets is the ruined 12th-century castle, the birthplace in 1512 of Catherine Parr, Henry VIII's last wife. The elegant 18th-century Abbott Hall preserves local traditions in the Museum of Lakeland Life and Industry

Refreshments

Plenty of choice in **Kendal**
Tea and coffee at farm at **Watchgate** *(east of the A6 north of Kendal)*
Eagle and Child PH♥, Station Inn PH,
Staveley
Brown Horse Inn PH, **Winster**
Hare and Hounds PH♥♥, **Bowland Bridge**
(just off the route)
Masons Arms PH♥♥, **Strawberry Bank**
(just off the route)
Punchbowl PH♥♥, **Crosthwaite**
Wheatsheaf PH♥, **Brigsteer**

Bowness-on-Windermere

Winster

Crosthwaite

Underbarrow

Brigsteer

Take care not to mistake the faded yellow line of the national park boundary for the solid yellow line of the route

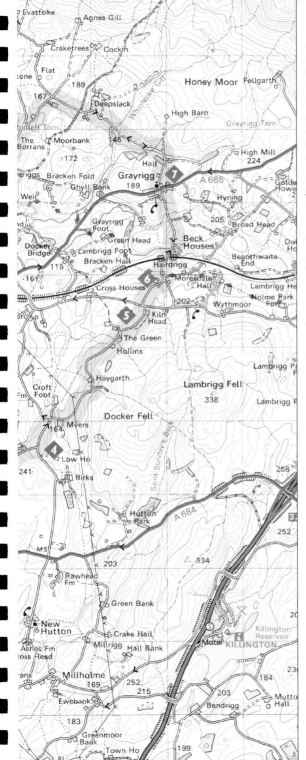

1 With back to the Tourist Information Centre R following the one-way system and signs for Sedbergh (A684). At T-j at the end of Castle Street bear R (in effect SA) 'A684 Sedbergh 9½' (the sign is on the wall to your right)

2 Ignore Sandylands Lane to your left. Shortly after passing allotments to your left, take the next proper L by a telephone box onto Sedbergh Road

3 Climb steeply. After 3 km (2 miles), and just before rejoining the main road turn L by a white cottage (NS)

4 At T-j L (NS). Continue downhill bearing R by Croft Foot Farm

5 At T-j just after Kiln Head Cottage L (NS) then R 'Moorfold, Thatchmoor Head'

6 At T-j / X-roads turn L towards cottage

7 At T-j with main road (A685) L then R by church 'Whinfell 3'

8 After 3 km (2 miles), immediately after crossing bridge turn R 'Selside, Watchgate 2'

9 At X-roads SA 'Watchgate 1'

10 At T-j with A6 L 'Kendal' then R 'Longsleddale 4½'

11 At bottom L over bridge 'Burnside 2½'

12 After 1½ km (1 mile) at top of short hill 1st R to continue uphill

13 At T-j after 2½ km (1½ miles) R 'Staveley'. Lovely wooded section

 next page

23 Through Brigsteer, climb steeply, descend to cross bridge over Kendal bypass. 5 km (3 miles) after Brigsteer, at X-roads on the edge of Kendal at the end of Brigsteer Road, SA. Shortly, at T-j R to return to the Tourist Information Centre

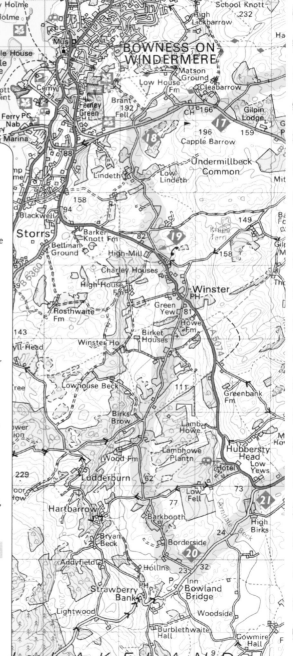

13 At T-j after 2½ km (1½ miles) R 'Staveley'. Lovely wooded section

14 At T-j with weir and small lake to the right turn L (NS). At X-roads with main road in Staveley SA 'Crook 2'

15 800 km (½ mile) after crossing the bridge over the main A591 1st R 'Sidegarth'

16 Through gates. At T-j R (NS)

17 Through more gates. After 4 km (2½ miles) at T-j with major road (B5284) R

18 After 1½ km (1 mile), shortly after X-roads sign 1st L 'Winster'

19 At T-j with main road (A5074) L then after 800 m (½ mile) 1st R opposite the Brown Horse Inn 'Bowland Bridge, Winster Church'

20 At T-j L (NS)

21 At T-j (with A5074) R 'Kendal, Lancaster' then on sharp RH bend 1st L 'Crosthwaite, Kendal'

22 Follow this road for 3 km (2 miles), passing through Crosthwaite. At the start of the village of Underbarrow turn R 'Milnthorpe, Levens. 6 ft 6 ins width limit'. After 800 m (½ mile), at T-j R 'Brigsteer, Levens'

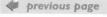 previous page

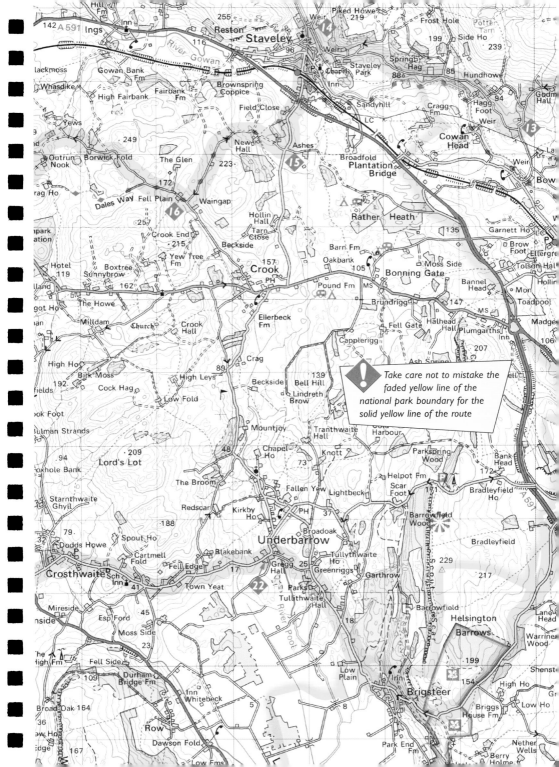

Take care not to mistake the faded yellow line of the national park boundary for the solid yellow line of the route

South from Kendal to Cartmel and Grange-over-Sands

Start

The Tourist Information Centre, Kendal

🅿 Follow signs for long-stay car parks

Distance and grade

53½ km (33½ miles)
Moderate

Terrain

Steep 106 m (350 ft) climb from Kendal onto Scout Scar above Brigsteer. Steep, then more gentle 173 m (570 ft) climb from Bowland Bridge south to Newton Fell. 94 m (310 ft) climb from Gilpin Bridge to above

*T*he fells to the east of Lake Windermere are little visited with the result that the roads are only lightly used – this more than anything else improves the enjoyment of the cycling. A steep climb that starts from right outside the Tourist Information Centre takes you around the southern end of Scout Scar to Underbarrow. From the crossing of the River Winster south of Crosthwaite, the route climbs steeply at first and then more gently onto Newton Fell with panoramic views opening up ahead and to the southeast. Cartmel is a real jewel of a village with several fine refreshment stops. Grange-over-Sands has the feel of a large town after so many miles of little-used lanes. The section that follows, although easy cycling and passing through attractive scenery, is neverthe-less affected by the noise of the busy A590, which is crossed via a small underpass near Town End, then joined very briefly near to Gilpin Bridge. Beyond Levens, you may be tempted to visit the Elizabethan Hall of Sizergh Castle with its lovely gardens. Two curiosities soon follow – the bridge carrying the A591 over the route near to Sizergh, which forms a wonderful echo chamber and then, the small wooden bridge over the River Kent just before Sedgwick. An easy lane through Sedgwick and Natland drops you near the start of the Kendal one-way system, which you follow back to the start.

Kendal   Brigsteer   Underbarrow   Crosthwaite   Cartmel Fell   High Newton

Levens. Highest point –
173 m (570 ft) on
Newton Fell near to
High Newton. Lowest
point – sea level at the
crossing of the River
Gilpin near Levens

 Nearest railway

Kendal

 Places of interest

Cartmel 7
Ivy-clad walls, old shops and pubs surround
the village square with its 18th-century
market cross. The magnificent priory
church, founded in 1188, has superb
stained-glass windows and choir stalls
carved with strange creatures. The 14th-
century gate-house was
once part of the priory

Levens Hall 16
Cones, corkscrews,
pyramids and other
curious shapes of fantastic
17th-century topiary
gardens are maintained in
their original forms. The grey-
stone hall was built in 1250
around the peel tower but the
building is mainly Elizabethan
with superb plaster-work and
carved woodwork. There is also
a working steam engine collection

Sizergh Castle 19
The medieval hall and Elizabethan
wings were added to the peel tower
built in 1350. There are many portraits and
relics of the Strickland family. Panelling,
original fireplaces and windows are to be
found in the tower museum and there are
rock, rose and Dutch gardens in the
grounds. The Queen's Room is named after
Catherine Parr, the sixth wife of Henry VIII

Refreshments

Plenty of choice in **Kendal**
Wheatsheaf PH ❦, **Brigsteer**
Punchbowl PH ❦❦, **Crosthwaite**
The Crown PH ❦, **High Newton**
Kings Arms PH ❦, *Cavendish Arms PH* ❦,
Pig and Whistle PH, **Cartmel**
Plenty of choice in **Grange-over-Sands**
Derby Arms PH, **Town End**
Gilpin Bridge Inn PH, **junction of A5074
and A590**
Hare and Hounds PH ❦❦, **Levens**
Strickland Arms PH ❦, **Sizergh**

Grange-over-Sands

Meathop

Levens

Natland

1 With back to the Tourist Information Centre SA uphill onto Allhallows Lane towards a large chimney. After 800 m (½ mile), opposite the Riflemans Arms PH L 'Scout Scar, Brigsteer, Lyth'. Shortly, at X-roads SA onto Brigsteer Road

2 *Easy to miss.* Follow this road for 7 km (4½ miles), climbing then descending through Brigsteer. 2½ km (1½ miles) after the Wheatsheaf PH in Brigsteer L 'Crosthwaite'. At T-j L 'Crosthwaite, Ulverston'. Shortly after the sign for Crosthwaite at start of village (near the Lyth Gallery) L opposite Guide Post Cottage 'Lancaster' then immediately R.

3 At X-roads with main road (A5074) SA 'Cartmel' '6 ft 6 ins width limit'

4 Climb, then descend. 2½ km (1½ miles) after the last X-roads, at the bottom of a hill 1st R by a triangle of grass 'Bowland Bridge' then shortly 1st L 'Cartmel Grange'

➡ **two pages**

14 At T-j with A590 L 'Cumbria Cycleway' then 1st L onto A5074 'Windermere, Bowness'

15 Go past the Gilpin Bridge Inn, ignore the 1st left to Bowness and Windermere. Continue towards dual carriageway, take the next L just after a garage on the left 'Cumbria Cycleway'

16 At T-j after 1 km (¾ mile) just after a bridge R 'Cumbria Cycleway' then at T-j after 50 m (yd) by the Hare and Hounds PH L towards the church

17 At X-roads by Levens Methodist Church leave the Cumbria Cycleway and continue SA (your priority)

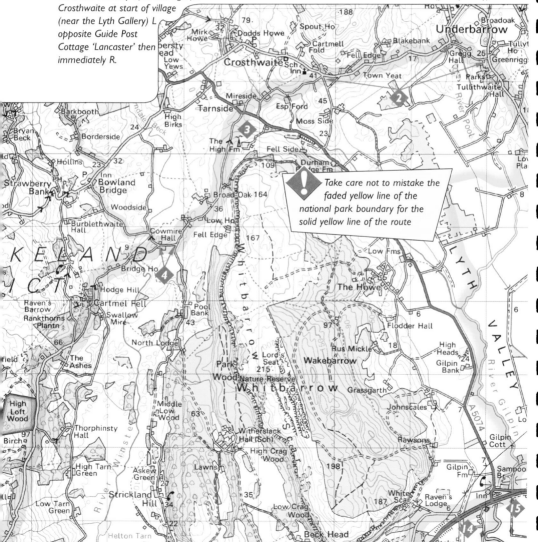

! Take care not to mistake the faded yellow line of the national park boundary for the solid yellow line of the route

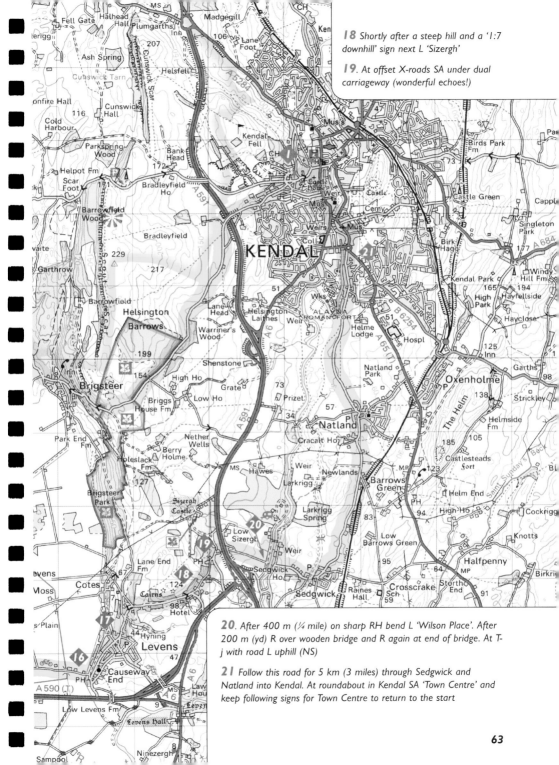

18 *Shortly after a steep hill and a '1:7 downhill' sign next L 'Sizergh'*

19. *At offset X-roads SA under dual carriageway (wonderful echoes!)*

20. *After 400 m (¼ mile) on sharp RH bend L 'Wilson Place'. After 200 m (yd) R over wooden bridge and R again at end of bridge. At T-j with road L uphill (NS)*

21 *Follow this road for 5 km (3 miles) through Sedgwick and Natland into Kendal. At roundabout in Kendal SA 'Town Centre' and keep following signs for Town Centre to return to the start*

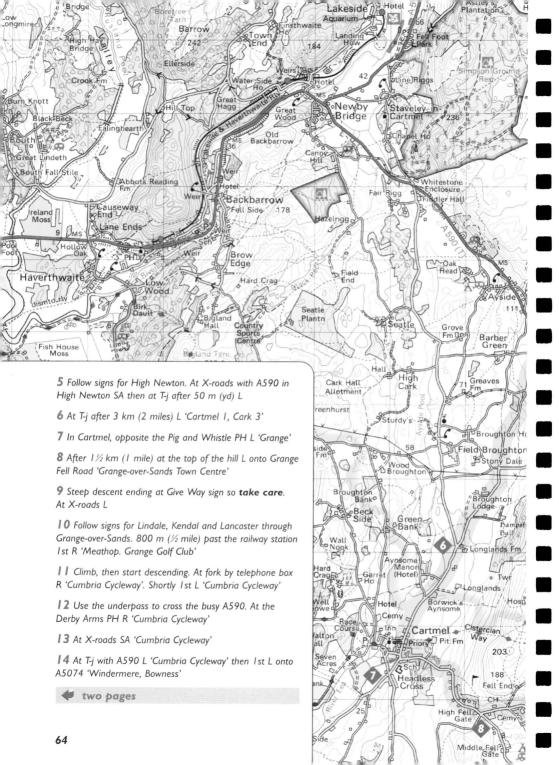

5 Follow signs for High Newton. At X-roads with A590 in High Newton SA then at T-j after 50 m (yd) L

6 At T-j after 3 km (2 miles) L 'Cartmel 1, Cark 3'

7 In Cartmel, opposite the Pig and Whistle PH L 'Grange'

8 After 1½ km (1 mile) at the top of the hill L onto Grange Fell Road 'Grange-over-Sands Town Centre'

9 Steep descent ending at Give Way sign so **take care**. At X-roads L

10 Follow signs for Lindale, Kendal and Lancaster through Grange-over-Sands. 800 m (½ mile) past the railway station 1st R 'Meathop. Grange Golf Club'

11 Climb, then start descending. At fork by telephone box R 'Cumbria Cycleway'. Shortly 1st L 'Cumbria Cycleway'

12 Use the underpass to cross the busy A590. At the Derby Arms PH R 'Cumbria Cycleway'

13 At X-roads SA 'Cumbria Cycleway'

14 At T-j with A590 L 'Cumbria Cycleway' then 1st L onto A5074 'Windermere, Bowness'

◀ two pages

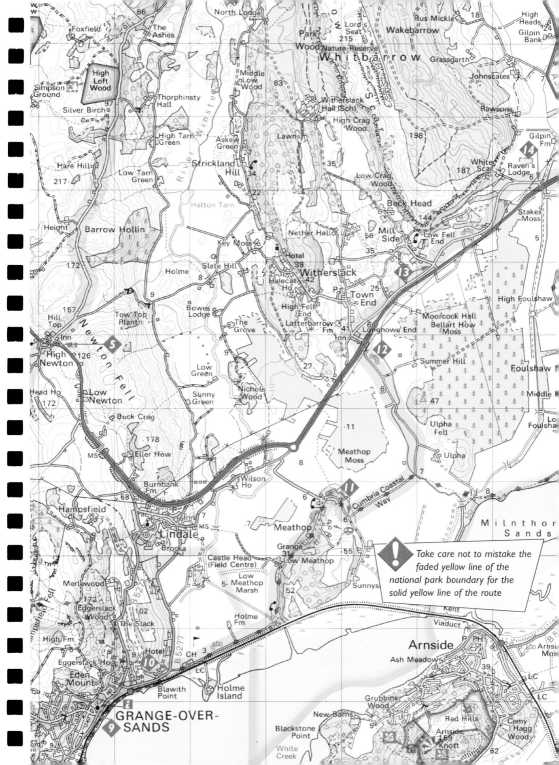

Take care not to mistake the faded yellow line of the national park boundary for the solid yellow line of the route

North to Sedbergh from Kirkby Lonsdale, returning via the Lune Valley

*T*he valley of the River Lune is the dominating feature of this ride, linking the attractive settlements of Kirkby Lonsdale and Sedbergh. Soon after leaving Kirkby, the route follows one of the tributaries of the Lune up the well-graded climb to the top of Barbondale, cutting through the westernmost

hills of the Pennines and offering fabulous valley views along Dentdale. After the climb to over 300 m (1000 ft), a steep descent takes you down into Dentdale with a delightful stretch along the River Dee. Sedbergh offers a wide variety of refreshments, which you may well need before the next two climbs – first to the heights of Winder, then, having descended into the

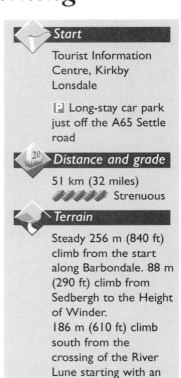

Start

Tourist Information Centre, Kirkby Lonsdale

P Long-stay car park just off the A65 Settle road

Distance and grade

51 km (32 miles)
🌶🌶🌶🌶🌶 Strenuous

Terrain

Steady 256 m (840 ft) climb from the start along Barbondale. 88 m (290 ft) climb from Sedbergh to the Height of Winder.
186 m (610 ft) climb south from the crossing of the River Lune starting with an

Lune Valley, a longer climb up to Fox's Pulpit. This second climb starts with two exceedingly steep sections near to the old railway viaduct. After Fox's Pulpit, a long, invigorating descent takes you down to the valley floor but remember to conserve enough energy for the last, unexpected climb that soon follows. This whole section, along the western side of the Lune Valley, is wonderful cycling country.

Kirkby Lonsdale   Casterton   Barbon Low Fell   Barbondale   Gawthrop   Sedbergh

 Refreshments

Snooty Fox PH 👜👜, *Sun PH* 👜👜, *plenty of choice in* **Kirkby Lonsdale**
Red Lion PH, Bull Hotel PH, Dalesman PH 👜👜, *tea shops in* **Sedbergh**

exceedingly steep section by the viaduct. Unexpected steep climb of 73 m (240 ft) halfway along Lune Valley. Highest point – 305 m (1000 ft) at the summit of Barbondale and also near Fox's Pulpit on the northern section of the ride. Lowest point – 39 m (130 ft) Kirkby Lonsdale

 Nearest railway

Wennington, 10 km (6 miles) south of the start

 Places of interest

Dent *(just off the route)* 6
Picturesque cobbled village overlooking the River Dee in Dentdale. Famous for its hand-knitted woollens, still produced by resident knitters at the nearby craft centre

Sedbergh 8
Lies beneath the domed peaks of the Howgill Fells where the Lune and Rawthey rivers meet. The playing fields of the public school, founded in 1525, flank the magnificent Norman church of St Andrew's

 ▼ *Sedbergh*

Howgill   Beck Foot   Fox's Pulpit   Killington   Kearstwick

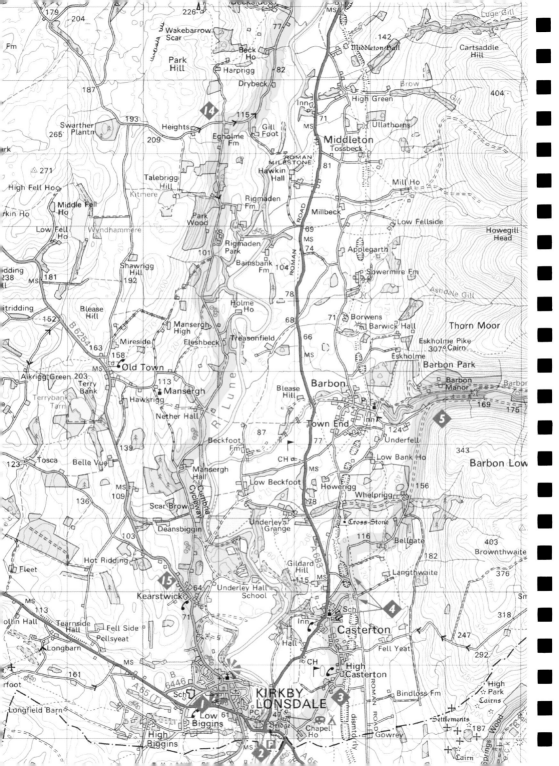

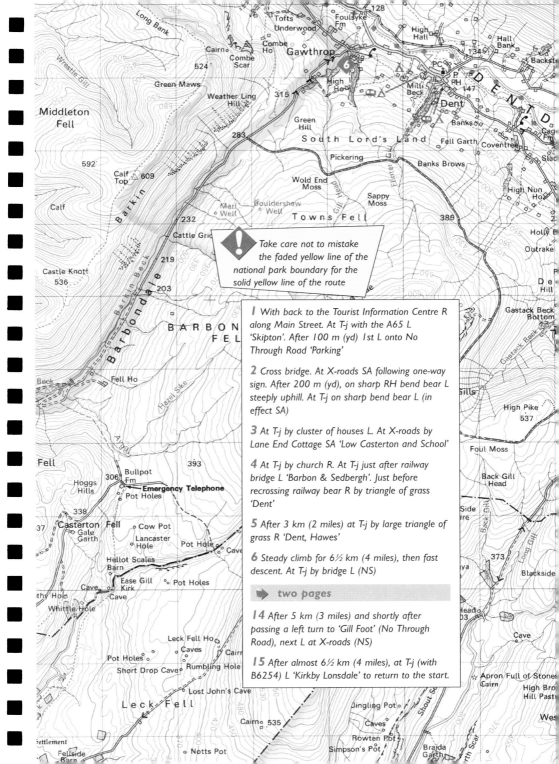

Take care not to mistake the faded yellow line of the national park boundary for the solid yellow line of the route

1 With back to the Tourist Information Centre R along Main Street. At T-j with the A65 L 'Skipton'. After 100 m (yd) 1st L onto No Through Road 'Parking'

2 Cross bridge. At X-roads SA following one-way sign. After 200 m (yd), on sharp RH bend bear L steeply uphill. At T-j on sharp bend bear L (in effect SA)

3 At T-j by cluster of houses L. At X-roads by Lane End Cottage SA 'Low Casterton and School'

4 At T-j by church R. At T-j just after railway bridge L 'Barbon & Sedbergh'. Just before recrossing railway bear R by triangle of grass 'Dent'

5 After 3 km (2 miles) at T-j by large triangle of grass R 'Dent, Hawes'

6 Steady climb for 6½ km (4 miles), then fast descent. At T-j by bridge L (NS)

➡ **two pages**

14 After 5 km (3 miles) and shortly after passing a left turn to 'Gill Foot' (No Through Road), next L at X-roads (NS)

15 After almost 6½ km (4 miles), at T-j (with B6254) L 'Kirkby Lonsdale' to return to the start.

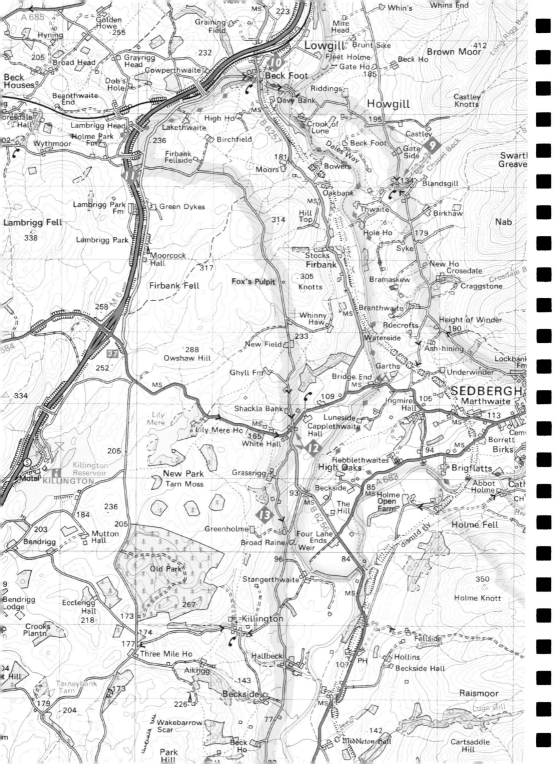

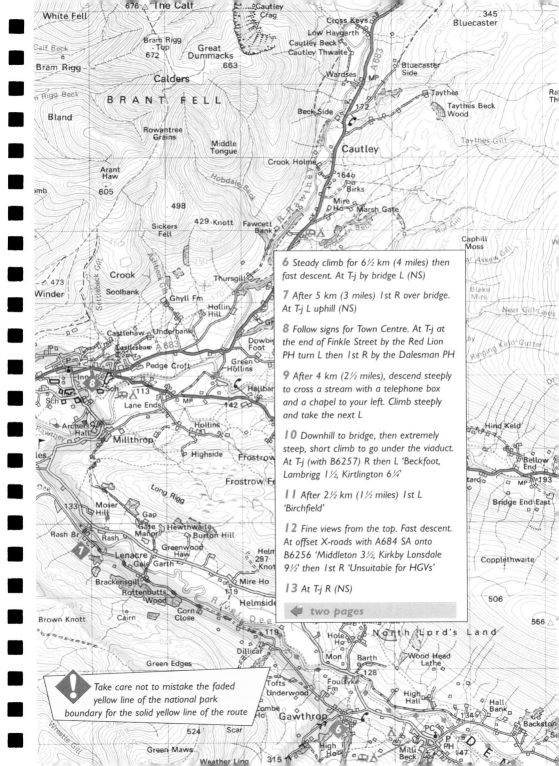

6 Steady climb for 6½ km (4 miles) then fast descent. At T-j by bridge L (NS)

7 After 5 km (3 miles) 1st R over bridge. At T-j L uphill (NS)

8 Follow signs for Town Centre. At T-j at the end of Finkle Street by the Red Lion PH turn L then 1st R by the Dalesman PH

9 After 4 km (2½ miles), descend steeply to cross a stream with a telephone box and a chapel to your left. Climb steeply and take the next L

10 Downhill to bridge, then extremely steep, short climb to go under the viaduct. At T-j (with B6257) R then L 'Beckfoot, Lambrigg 1½, Kirtlington 6¼'

11 After 2½ km (1½ miles) 1st L 'Birchfield'

12 Fine views from the top. Fast descent. At offset X-roads with A684 SA onto B6256 'Middleton 3½, Kirkby Lonsdale 9½' then 1st R 'Unsuitable for HGVs'

13 At T-j R (NS)

◄ two pages

Take care not to mistake the faded yellow line of the national park boundary for the solid yellow line of the route

South from Kirkby Lonsdale above the River Lune and east to Wray and Low Bentham

12

Three counties are visited during the course of this ride – Kirkby Lonsdale lies just inside Cumbria, but you soon cross into Lancashire and stay in this county for most of the ride with the exception of a 5 km (3 miles) section north of Low Bentham within North Yorkshire's boundaries. The ride heads south along the valley of the River Lune to Newton, after which quiet lanes take you out of the valley to Over Kellet before joining the magnificent ridge high above the valley bottom with wonderful views across to the moors to the east. The Lune is crossed at Loyn Bridge near to Hornby, the first of a succession of small villages along the course of the route, each with solid stone-built houses and a local hostelry. There is a last, lovely section through Ireby and Leck before a short, unavoidable 3 km (2 miles) of the busy A65. The first 800 m (½ mile) is the worst – you soon have a white line to separate you from the traffic on your return to the start.

|74| Kirkby Lonsdale |75|
|76| |77|

Start

Tourist Information Centre, Kirkby Lonsdale

P Long-stay car park just off the A65 Settle road

Distance and grade

46½ km (29 miles)

Moderate

Terrain

128 m (420 ft) climb from the River Keer near Capernwray south to the ridge above Aughton. 91 m (300 ft) climb from the River Lune near Hornby to the hill between Wray and Low Bentham. 61 m (200 ft) climb from Burton in Lonsdale to Leck. Highest point – 144 m (475 ft) on the ridge above Aughton. Lowest point – 21 m (70 ft) at the bridge over the River Lune near Hornby

Nearest railway

Wennington, 3 km (2 miles) north of the route at Wray

Kirkby Lonsdale   Whittington   Docker Park   Capernwray   Over Kellet

Kirkby Lonsdale 1

Georgian buildings and quaint cottages combine in the riverside 'capital' of the Lune valley. The views from the churchyard were praised by Ruskin as 'naturally divine' and painted by Turner. There are two bridges over the River Lune, an ancient one called Devil's Bridge, supposedly built by Satan, and a new one built in 1932. It is said that when Satan put up his bridge, he claimed the first living thing to cross it – which turned out to be an old dog

▼ *Devil's Bridge, Kirkby Lonsdale*

Hornby 12

Gargoyles on the battlements of Hornby Castle grimace down on the village, which is divided by the River Wenning. Below the castle, Hornby's main street leads down from the 19th-century Church of St Margaret to the three-arched stone bridge across the River Wenning. The street is bordered by Georgian houses and cottages and the Royal Oak Inn bears the names of its original owners, William and Emma Gelderd, with the date 1781

Gressingham Hornby Wray Low Bentham Burton in Lonsdale

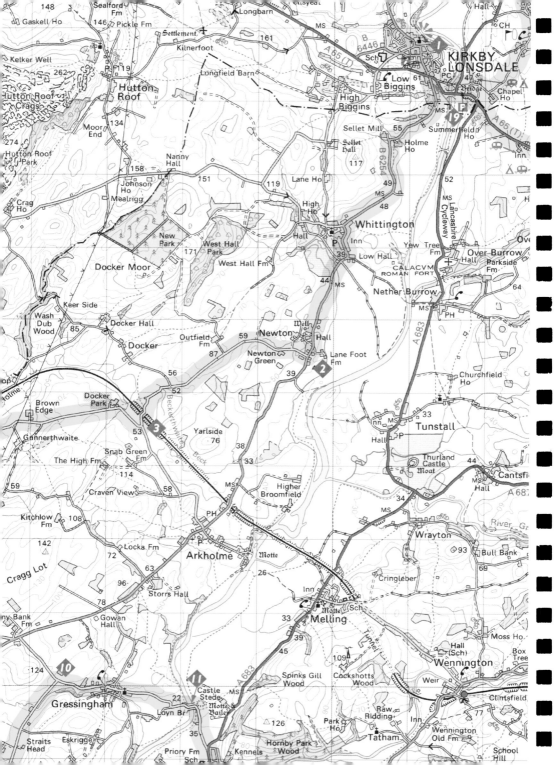

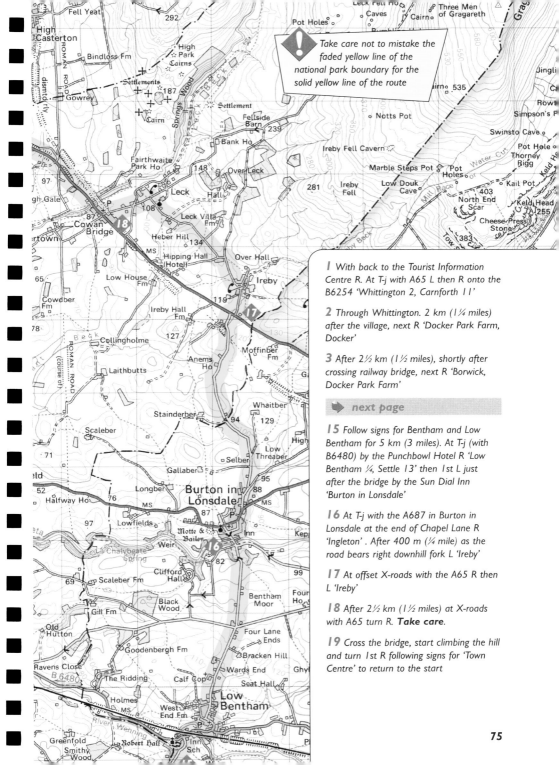

Take care not to mistake the faded yellow line of the national park boundary for the solid yellow line of the route

1 With back to the Tourist Information Centre R. At T-j with A65 L then R onto the B6254 'Whittington 2, Carnforth 11'

2 Through Whittington. 2 km (1¼ miles) after the village, next R 'Docker Park Farm, Docker'

3 After 2½ km (1½ miles), shortly after crossing railway bridge, next R 'Borwick, Docker Park Farm'

➡ next page

15 Follow signs for Bentham and Low Bentham for 5 km (3 miles). At T-j (with B6480) by the Punchbowl Hotel R 'Low Bentham ¼, Settle 13' then 1st L just after the bridge by the Sun Dial Inn 'Burton in Lonsdale'

16 At T-j with the A687 in Burton in Lonsdale at the end of Chapel Lane R 'Ingleton' . After 400 m (¼ mile) as the road bears right downhill fork L 'Ireby'

17 At offset X-roads with the A65 R then L 'Ireby'

18 After 2½ km (1½ miles) at X-roads with A65 turn R. **Take care**.

19 Cross the bridge, start climbing the hill and turn 1st R following signs for 'Town Centre' to return to the start

3 After 2½ km (1½ miles), shortly after crossing railway bridge, next R 'Borwick, Docker Park Farm'

4 At T-j after 4 km (2½ miles) L 'Capernwray, Arkholme'

5 After 1 km (¾ mile) 1st R opposite church 'Capernwray House'

6 At X-roads (with B6254) in Over Kellet SA 'Nether Kellet 2'

7 After 1 km (¾ mile) at the top of the hill opposite the neat stone wall of 'Challonaise' 1st L

8 At T-j L (NS) then 1st R (NS)

9 (Do not confuse with previous instruction!) At T-j R (NS) then 1st L 'Aughton'

10 Superb views into Lune Valley. At T-j after 5 km (3 miles) R 'Gressingham ½, Hornby 2'

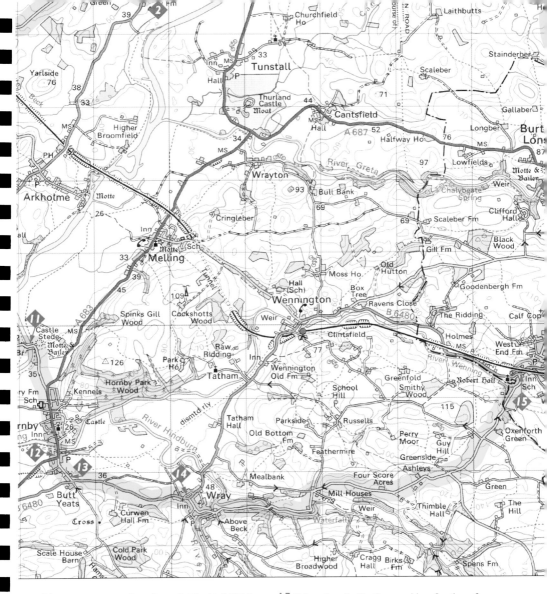

11 Cross bridge over River Lune. At T-j with A683 R 'Lancaster'

12 Through Hornby. Cross bridge over river. On sharp RH bend next L 'Bentham 6¼, Wray 1¼'

13 At X-roads with B6480 L 'Wray, Bentham'.

14 Shortly after the New Inn in Wray 1st R 'Higher Tatham, Lowgill'

15 Follow signs for Bentham and Low Bentham for 5 km (3 miles). At T-j (with B6480) by the Punchbowl Hotel R 'Low Bentham ¼, Settle 13' then 1st L just after the bridge by the Sun Dial Inn 'Burton in Lonsdale'

◀ **two pages**

South from Hawkshead to the southern end of Lake Windermere, returning via Coniston Water

Heavy tourist traffic in the heart of the Lake District makes most roads among the central fells unsuitable for leisure cycling at all but at the quietest times of the day or year. This ride goes as close to the central fells as possible on lightly used roads. However, even here, it is best to avoid the busiest times of the year. Starting at Hawkshead, the ride follows the eastern side of first Esthwaite Water, then Lake Windermere, and the lake is occasionally glimpsed through the trees. A steep climb onto the ridge above the lake takes you past Graythwaite Hall, then Bobbin Mill, the sole survivor of the local bobbin factories. A descent into the unexpected flat and tidal Rusland Valley is followed by a climb over the hill into the valley of the River Crake, which drains Coniston Water. This is the loveliest stretch of the ride with spectacular views across Coniston Water to the fells behind. There are no black arrows on the map but the climb from the end of the lake to the B5285 and on to High Cross is the longest and most sustained of the ride. The good side of this is that you are left with a fine, fast descent back to the start.

Start

Tourist Information Centre, Hawkshead, 8 km (5 miles) south-west of Ambleside

P Follow signs for long-stay car park. Arrive early during busy holiday periods

Distance and grade

43 km (27 miles)
Moderate

Terrain

Two climbs, both steep: 64 m (210 ft) from Lake Windermere to Graythwaite Hall.

Hawkshead   Near Sawrey   Graythwaite Hall   Finsthwaite

Places of interest

Hawkshead 1
A medieval village with a maze of alleys. The church and the courthouse are 15th-century. William Heelis had his solicitor's office in Thimble Hall when he married Beatrix Potter and the Hall now houses an exhibition of her life and work

Hill Top 3
Scenes from Peter Rabbit come alive in the 17th-century farmhouse that inspired Beatrix Potter's work. She bought it as her retreat in 1905 and it is now preserved by the National Trust

Stott Park Bobbin Mill 6
The sole survivor of the local bobbin factories. Opened in 1835 and still in working order, it is now a museum of social and industrial history

Brantwood 13
The Coniston home, built in 1797, of the Victorian artist and writer John Ruskin from 1872 to 1900. The study, dining room and bedroom are much as he left them, full of drawings and artistic treasures; the grounds include a nature trail

Refreshments

Kings Arms PH 🍴🍴, *Queens Head* 🍴🍴, *plenty of choice in* **Hawkshead**
Tower Bank Arms PH 🍴🍴, **Near Sawrey**
Sawrey Hotel PH 🍴🍴, **Far Sawrey**
White Hart PH, **Bouth**
Royal Oak PH, **Spark Bridge**

155 m (510 ft) from Coniston Water to High Cross above Hawkshead. Highest point – 199 m (655 ft) at High Cross, above Hawkshead. Lowest point – sea level at the crossing of Rusland Pool near Bouth

Nearest railway

Windermere, 5 km (3 miles) from the route at Far Sawrey (via the ferry)

Spark Bridge

High Nibthwaite

Brantwood

Hawkshead Hill

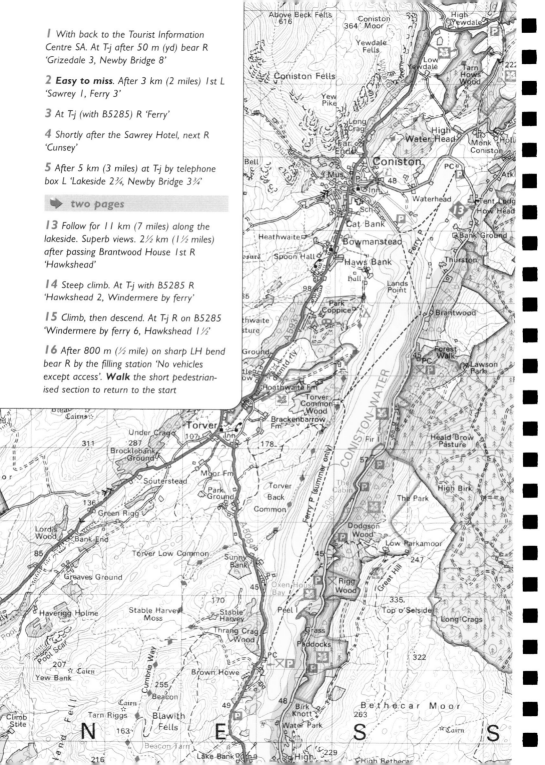

1 With back to the Tourist Information Centre SA. At T-j after 50 m (yd) bear R 'Grizedale 3, Newby Bridge 8'

2 **Easy to miss**. After 3 km (2 miles) 1st L 'Sawrey 1, Ferry 3'

3 At T-j (with B5285) R 'Ferry'

4 Shortly after the Sawrey Hotel, next R 'Cunsey'

5 After 5 km (3 miles) at T-j by telephone box L 'Lakeside 2¾, Newby Bridge 3¾'

➡ **two pages**

13 Follow for 11 km (7 miles) along the lakeside. Superb views. 2½ km (1½ miles) after passing Brantwood House 1st R 'Hawkshead'

14 Steep climb. At T-j with B5285 R 'Hawkshead 2, Windermere by ferry'

15 Climb, then descend. At T-j R on B5285 'Windermere by ferry 6, Hawkshead 1½'

16 After 800 m (½ mile) on sharp LH bend bear R by the filling station 'No vehicles except access'. **Walk** the short pedestrianised section to return to the start

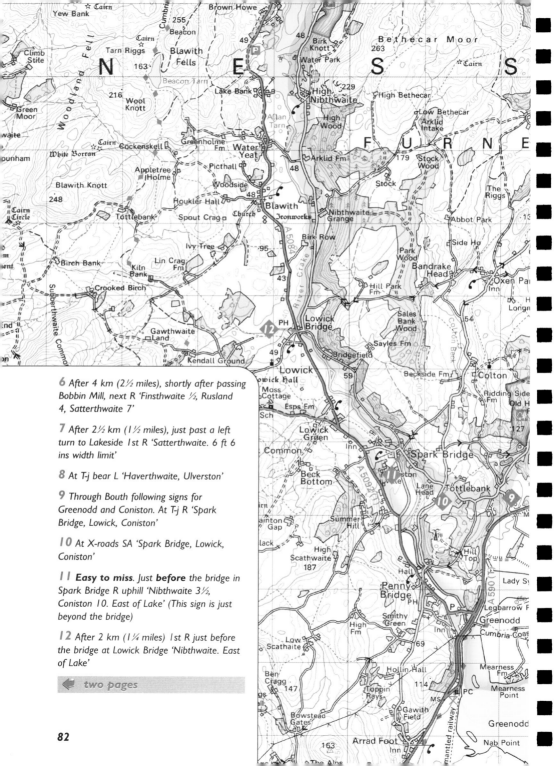

6 After 4 km (2½ miles), shortly after passing Bobbin Mill, next R 'Finsthwaite ½, Rusland 4, Satterthwaite 7'

7 After 2½ km (1½ miles), just past a left turn to Lakeside 1st R 'Satterthwaite. 6 ft 6 ins width limit'

8 At T-j bear L 'Haverthwaite, Ulverston'

9 Through Bouth following signs for Greenodd and Coniston. At T-j R 'Spark Bridge, Lowick, Coniston'

10 At X-roads SA 'Spark Bridge, Lowick, Coniston'

11 **Easy to miss**. Just **before** the bridge in Spark Bridge R uphill 'Nibthwaite 3½, Coniston 10. East of Lake' (This sign is just beyond the bridge)

12 After 2 km (1¼ miles) 1st R just before the bridge at Lowick Bridge 'Nibthwaite. East of Lake'

◄ *two pages*

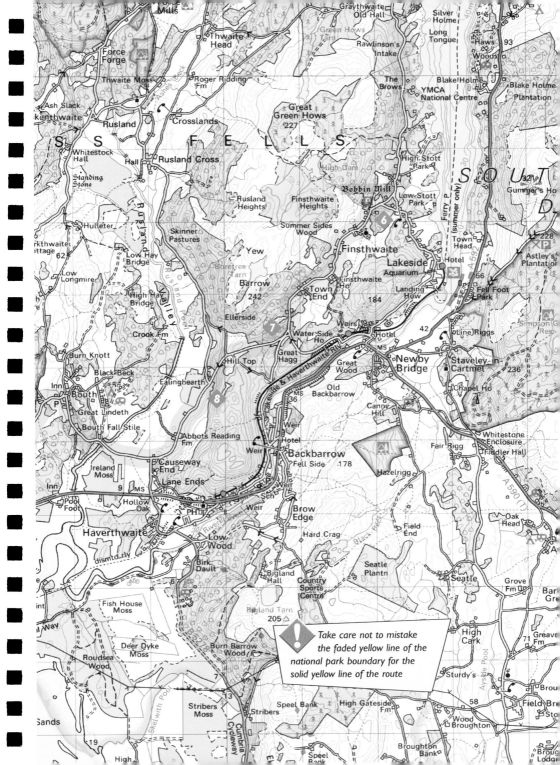

Take care not to mistake the faded yellow line of the national park boundary for the solid yellow line of the route

14 *Over steep fells to Ravenglass northwest from Broughton in Furness*

This is a reasonably tough ride with over 910 m (3000 ft) of climbing, at times very steep. It takes in the little-visited south-western corner of the Lake District, starting from the attractive, solid village of Broughton in Furness. The first 5 km (3 miles) present few problems enabling you to appreciate the quin-tessential Lakeland beauty of the valley of the charmingly named River Lickle with its glades, stonewalls, streams and stone hamlets. Soon after the pub in Broughton Mills, the first major hill is encountered. A fast descent to the River Duddon at Hall Dunnerdale is followed by a gentle section along the valley floor. Make the most of it! The 1 in 4 sign at the bottom of the hill tells no lies: the first section is very steep. The open moorland of Birker Fell is traversed leading to the easy middle section in the valleys of the Rivers Esk and Mite. You descend to the sea at Ravenglass, crossing a footbridge over the estuary next to the railway line. Ravenglass was much loved by smugglers in centuries past. An unavoidable 5 km (3 mile) section on the busy A595 must be endured before the final, and hardest challenge up over Corney Fell.

Start

The square, Broughton in Furness, 16 km (10 miles) southwest of Coniston

P In the square in Broughton in Furness

Distance and grade

54 km (34 miles)

///// Highly strenuous

Terrain

Hilly, with 3 major climbs and two shorter ones. 70 m (230 ft) north from Broughton at the start. 222m (730 ft) from Broughton Mills to the pass over Dunnerdale Fells. 192 m (630 ft) from Ulpha to the pass

[map grid showing 88, 89, 86, 87]

[elevation profile with labels: Broughton in Furness, Lower Hawthwaite, Broughton Mills, Hall Dunnerdale, Ulpha, Birker Fell, Eskdale Green] over Birker Fell (including a very steep 1:4 section at the start). 79 m (260 ft) climb from Ravenglass to Muncaster Castle. 405 m (1330 ft) climb from crossing the River Esk to the pass over Thwaites Fell with some very steep sections. Highest point – 405 m (1330 ft) on Thwaites Fell. Lowest point – sea level at Ravenglass

Nearest railway

Foxfield, 2½ km (1½ miles) south of the route at the start or Ravenglass (on the route)

Places of interest

Broughton in Furness 1
The village has a market overlooking the Duddon estuary. The Market Square has stone-slab stalls and a 1766 clock. Broughton Tower is a 14th-century peel tower, incorporated into the 18th-century house

Ravenglass 10
Lies on an estuary where three rivers – the Esk, the Mite and the Irt – enter the sea, and for a long while its sheltered position made it an important harbour. The Romans used it and, in the 2nd-century, built the large fort of Glannaventa on the cliffs above. In the 18th century, Ravenglass was much used as a base for smuggling contraband tobacco and French brandy from the Isle of Man. The century-old miniature railway was once used to carry minerals and now takes tourists on a scenic 11 km (7 mile) trip up Eskdale

Muncaster Castle 11
Home of the Pennington family since the 13th-century, it was a sanctuary for Henry VI during the Wars of the Roses. There is an owl aviary and rhododendron gardens

Refreshments

Plenty of choice in **Broughton in Furness**
Blacksmith Arms PH, **Broughton Mills**
King George IV PH ●, Bower House
Inn PH ●●, **Eskdale Green**
Ratty Arms PH ●, **Ravenglass**

Most sheep are stupid; those that live on Thwaites Fell on the long fast descent back to the start are not only stupid but also suicidal and likely to leap out of a ditch to throw themselves under your wheels without any provocation – resist the temptation to break the land speed record on this stretch and never lose your concentration.

Ravenglass   Broad Oak   Corney Fell   Thwaites Fell   Duddon Bridge

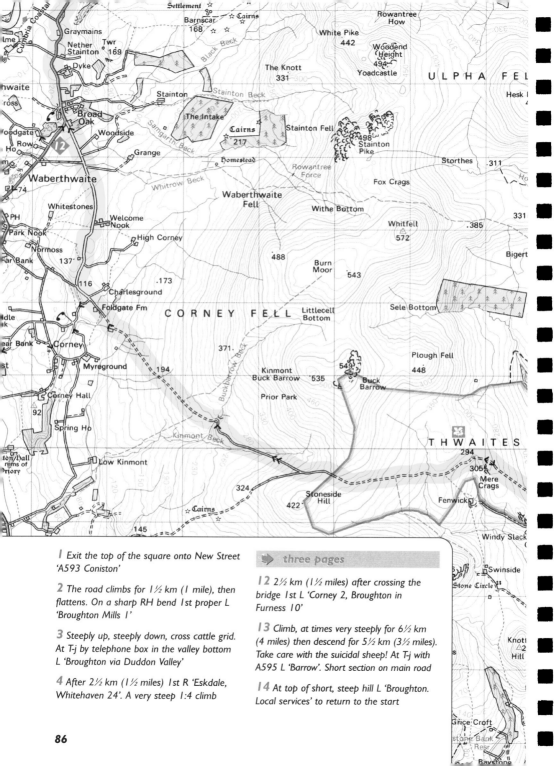

1 Exit the top of the square onto New Street 'A593 Coniston'

2 The road climbs for 1½ km (1 mile), then flattens. On a sharp RH bend 1st proper L 'Broughton Mills 1'

3 Steeply up, steeply down, cross cattle grid. At T-j by telephone box in the valley bottom L 'Broughton via Duddon Valley'

4 After 2½ km (1½ miles) 1st R 'Eskdale, Whitehaven 24'. A very steep 1:4 climb

➡ *three pages*

12 2½ km (1½ miles) after crossing the bridge 1st L 'Corney 2, Broughton in Furness 10'

13 Climb, at times very steeply for 6½ km (4 miles) then descend for 5½ km (3½ miles). Take care with the suicidal sheep! At T-j with A595 L 'Barrow'. Short section on main road

14 At top of short, steep hill L 'Broughton. Local services' to return to the start

Take care not to mistake the faded yellow line of the national park boundary for the solid yellow line of the route

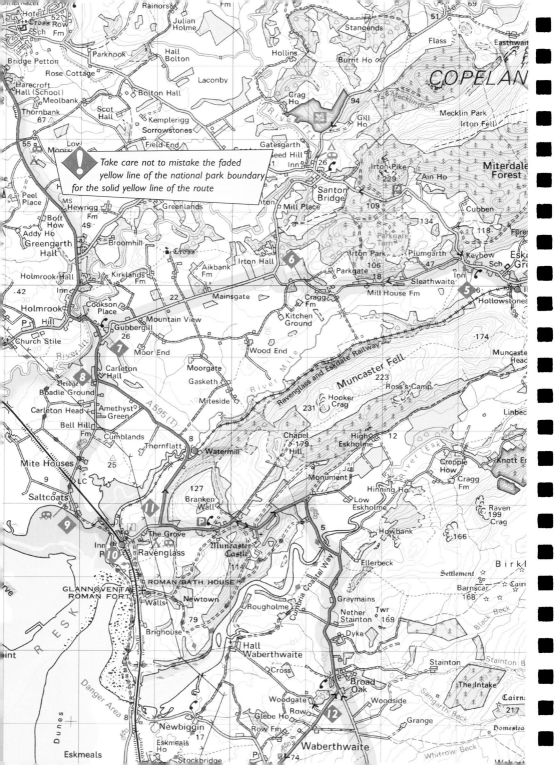

Take care not to mistake the faded yellow line of the national park boundary for the solid yellow line of the route

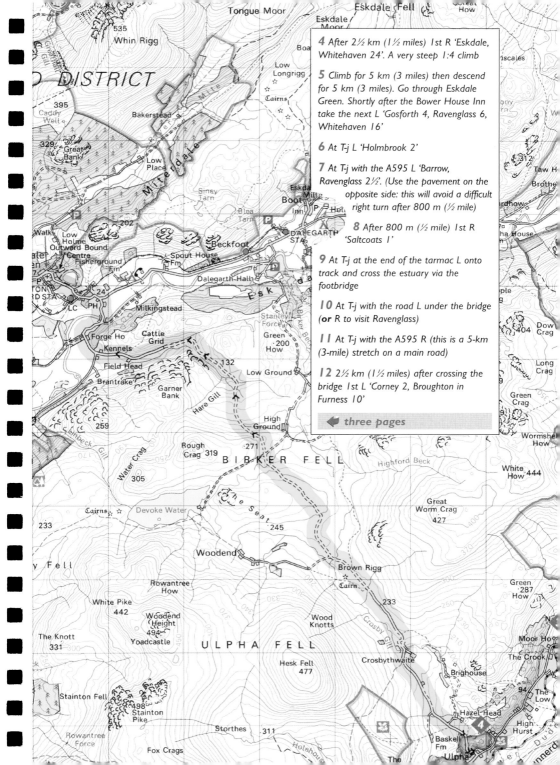

4 After 2½ km (1½ miles) 1st R 'Eskdale, Whitehaven 24'. A very steep 1:4 climb

5 Climb for 5 km (3 miles) then descend for 5 km (3 miles). Go through Eskdale Green. Shortly after the Bower House Inn take the next L 'Gosforth 4, Ravenglass 6, Whitehaven 16'

6 At T-j L 'Holmbrook 2'

7 At T-j with the A595 L 'Barrow, Ravenglass 2½'. (Use the pavement on the opposite side: this will avoid a difficult right turn after 800 m (½ mile)

8 After 800 m (½ mile) 1st R 'Saltcoats 1'

9 At T-j at the end of the tarmac L onto track and cross the estuary via the footbridge

10 At T-j with the road L under the bridge (**or** R to visit Ravenglass)

11 At T-j with the A595 R (this is a 5-km (3-mile) stretch on a main road)

12 2½ km (1½ miles) after crossing the bridge 1st L 'Corney 2, Broughton in Furness 10'

three pages

Tour of the Caldbeck and Uldake Fells from Bassenthwaite

A classic ride at the northern edge of the Lake District, starting from the attractive village of Bassenthwaite and climbing steadily for 396 m (1300 ft) first on road, then on a good stone-based track past the delights of Dash Waterfalls. The gradient is steep enough for some short pushing sections. Skiddaw House used to be an old shepherd's hut and is now a youth hostel. The next section is slow and may be boggy and/or rough. Once the track improves, you are rewarded with a very fine descent all the way to the improbably situated Quakers coffee shop in Mosedale, a very welcome stop. The second climb is on road as far as Calebreck. Unfortunately, the old mining road contouring the northern edge of the Caldbeck Fells is not a right of way, which is a pity as it would be an ideal track for off-road riding. Instead, you must descend to Hesket Newmarket before climbing back up to Fell Side. There is one last off-road section between the farms at Howburn and Longlands. The views of Skiddaw along the final road section are magnificent and a gentle descent down to Bassenthwaite is a well-deserved reward at the end of the ride.

Start

The Sun PH, Bassenthwaite, 10 km (6 miles) north of Keswick

P No specific car park. Please ask for permission if you use the pub car park or alternatively park along the tree-lined avenue in the village of Bassenthwaite

Distance and grade

38 km (24 miles)
///// Strenuous

Terrain

In general good surface on quiet lanes or stone-based tracks. One boggy / rough section for about 2½ km (1½ miles) northeast from Skiddaw House. Two main climbs – 396 m (1300 ft) from Bassenthwaite to above Dash Waterfalls, parts of which will require pushing, 183 m (600 ft) of climbing in two

Bassenthwaite   Dead Crags   Skiddaw House   Roundhouse   Mosedale

sections between Hesket Newmarket and Longlands. Highest point – 497 m (1630 feet) above Dash Waterfalls. Lowest point – 100 m (330 feet) at the start in Bassenthwaite

Nearest railway

Penrith, 19 km (12 miles) east of the route at Mose-dale or Aspatria, 13 km (8 miles) northwest of the route at Bassenthwaite

Places of interest

Bassenthwaite 1
There are traces of Roman and Norse settlements around the village

Hesket Newmarket 9
The open-sided market building on the village green survives from days of sheep and cattle trading

Caldbeck (just off the route) 10
John Peel was buried here after falling from his horse in 1854, aged 78. The river-powered woollen mills once produced grey cloth for Peel's hunting coats. The wheel still turns on the restored 18th-century Priests Mill

Skiddaw 14
The mountain is one of only four peaks in England that rise to over 910 m (3000 ft); the other three are also in the Lake District – Scafell, Scafell Pike and Helvellyn

Refreshments

The Sun PH 🍺🍺, **Bassenthwaite**
Quaker Coffee House, **Mosedale**
Mill Inn PH 🍺, **Mungrisdale** *(just off the route south of Mosedale)*
Old Crown PH 🍺🍺, **Hesket Newmarket**

Hesket Newmarket   Branthwaite   Longlands   Orthwaite

1 With back to The Sun PH turn L then 1st R over the bridge

2 Climb steadily. At T-j R 'Keswick 8'

3 Descend to the stream and start climbing. After 1 km (¾ mile), shortly after the brow of the hill L onto tarmac lane 'Public Bridleway. Skiddaw House and Threlkeld via Dash Falls'

4 Climb on tarmac through several gates. After 1½ km (1 mile) 1st major track R by a cairn of stones 'Bridleway via Dash Falls. Skiddaw House. Threlkeld'

5 Gradient steepens. Some short pushing sections. Past falls, over the brow, then descend and climb to Skiddaw House. Just before the house L downhill by wall on grassy slope

6 This section is in parts boggy and for the next 2½ km (1½ miles), you will be faced with a mixture of cycling and pushing. The surface improves, then turns to tarmac

7 At T-j with road L

8 2½ km (1½ miles) after passing through Mosedale, just past a chevron sign turn L onto fell road

9 At T-j at bottom of hill L 'Hesket Newmarket ½, Caldbeck 2'

10 At the end of the village, on a sharp RH bend, bear L between houses (NS)

11 After 2½ km (1½ miles), at top of hill, turn L 'Fell Side, Branthwaite, Green Head'

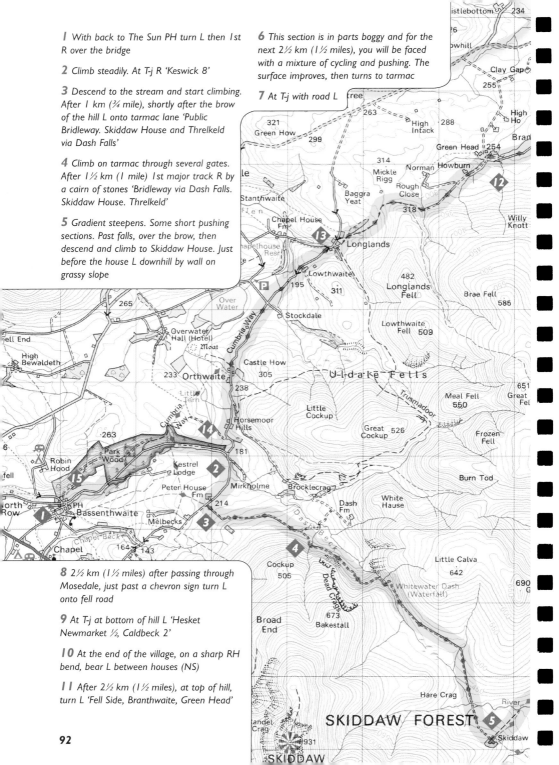

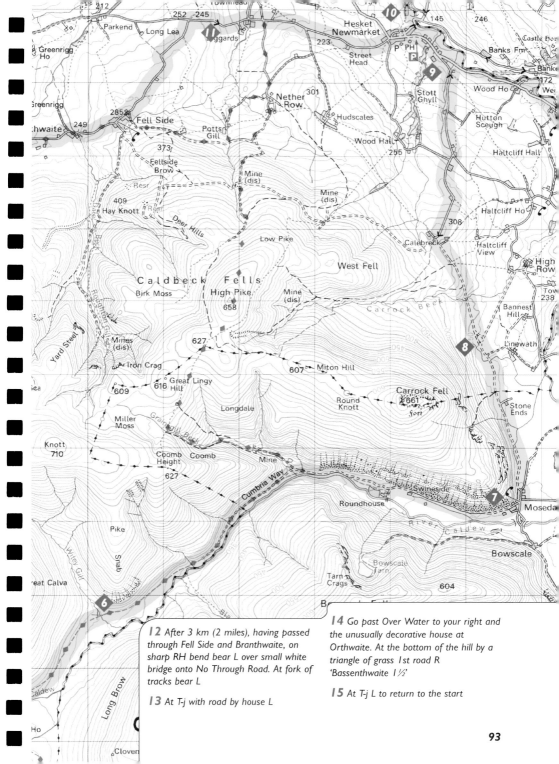

12 After 3 km (2 miles), having passed through Fell Side and Branthwaite, on sharp RH bend bear L over small white bridge onto No Through Road. At fork of tracks bear L

13 At T-j with road by house L

14 Go past Over Water to your right and the unusually decorative house at Orthwaite. At the bottom of the hill by a triangle of grass 1st road R 'Bassenthwaite 1½'

15 At T-j L to return to the start

Along the Allerdale Ramble east from Cockermouth

Starting from the handsome town of Cockermouth, the ride heads east on roads along the valley of the River Derwent for almost 11 km (7 miles), passing the attractive house at Hewthwaite Hall and heading towards ever closer views of the fells lying to the east, notably Binsey, the Uldake Fells and the great bulk of Skiddaw. The off-road riding starts at Irton House with a short section of fields and gates before the going improves on good tracks through forestry. The route descends to the road near Castle Inn and joins the course of the Allerdale Ramble, which it follows all the way back to Cockermouth, starting with a stretch alongside the River Derwent, which may be muddy in parts after wet weather. The longest climb of the ride and the best descent starts after the crossing of the River Derwent near Isel. Almost 150 m (500 ft) of ascent through woods, then fields bring you to the top of Watch Hill with the long, grassy descent back to Cockermouth spread out before you.

Start

Earl Mayo's statue, High Street, Cockermouth

P Several pay and display car parks in Cockermouth

Distance and grade

24 km (15 miles)
Easy/moderate

Terrain

A short section near to the River Derwent may become muddy after wet weather. 100 m (330 ft) climb from crossing the River Derwent to the start of the off-road section at Irton House. 143 m (470 ft) climb from the river up to the top of Watch Hill. Highest point – 213 m (700 ft) at the top of Watch Hill. Lowest point – 42 m (140 ft) at the start

Nearest railway

Maryport, 11 km (7 miles) northwest of Cockermouth

Cockermouth   Hewthwaite Hall   River Derwent   Irton House

► *The River Derwent*

Places of interest

Cockermouth 1

William Wordsworth was born in a
Georgian house at the end of the main
street. There are the remains of a largely
14th-century castle at the junction of the
Cocker and Derwent rivers

Refreshments

*Brown Cow PH ♥, plenty of choice
in* **Cockermouth**
Castle Inn PH, **Kilnhill**

Castle Inn

River Derwent

Watch Hill

1 With back to the Bush PH (near to the statue) R along the main street following signs for the Sports Centre up Castle Gate

2 At the edge of town 1st major L onto Isel Road 'Hospital, Isel 3'

3 After 5 km (3 miles) 1st road L 'Blindcrake 1¾, Sunderland 2¼'. Cross bridge, then immediatley R 'Sunderland, Bewaldeth'

4 Ignore 1st right on sharp LH bend (No Through Road). Take next road R 'Bewaldeth'

5 Under pylons, SA at X-roads (your priority) then shortly after brow of hill R onto track towards Irton House Farm 'Public Bridleway. Castle Inn'. Opposite 1st house on right turn L through gate (blue arrow) aiming for corner of yard

6 Through gate and turn L following fence to the end of the field. Exit field via gate and keep fence to your right. At the end of this field turn R through gate to continue on a course at right angles to previous direction

7 Soon join better track. Follow this past ruin and through gate onto stone track. At X-roads of tracks L through Forestry Commission gate onto forest road

8 At fork stay on upper LH track

9 At T-j with road R for 400 m (¼ mile) then on sharp LH bend R onto No Through Road (to the R of Hotel Entrance)

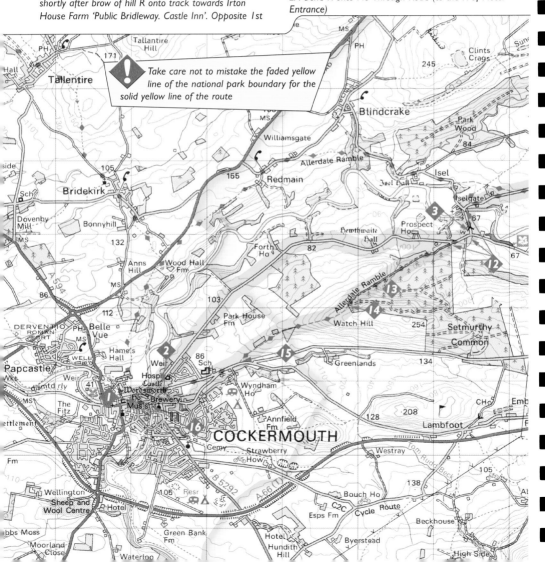

Take care not to mistake the faded yellow line of the national park boundary for the solid yellow line of the route

10 As tarmac drive swings right bear L (in effect SA) through bridgegate 'Public Bridleway to Isel'

11 Follow this track, at times excellent and at times muddy, in the same direction and through farm. At road bear L (in effect SA)

12 At T-j L over bridge 'Cockermouth'. Climb steeply. At T-j R 'Cockermouth 3¼'. After 400 m (¼ mile) near brow of hill bear L through wide wooden gate onto broad stone track

13 At fork of tracks at edge of deciduous wood bear R uphill

14 Exit wood via green metal gate on to grassy track climbing through field

15 Climb, then superb, long, grassy descent. At T-j with road R then 1st road L just past drive to Wyndham House

16 At T-j in the centre of Cockermouth L to return to the start

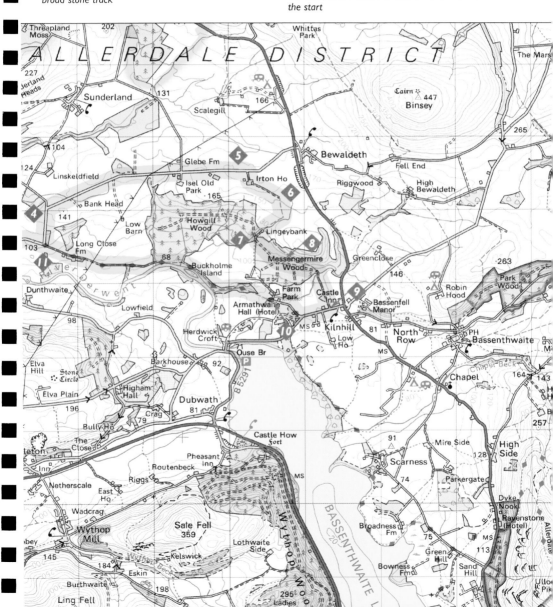

3 North from Loweswater over Mosser Fell

Although this ride spends the majority of its length on metalled roads, the lanes in question have at their start signs of 'Unsuitable for motors' or 'Unfit for cars', which means that you will have them to yourself. The other benefit of this is that the ride is an all-year round route, which will hardly deteriorate after wet weather or in the winter. The ride starts from the bottom of Scale Hill at the north end of Crummock Water and in the first section, there are fabulous views to savour, southeast down the Buttermere valley towards the very heart of the Central Fells. Nearer to hand lies the dramatic lump of Melbreak rising almost 460 m (1500 ft) above Crummock Water. Loweswater is almost circumnavigated first on tracks through woodland, then along the lakeside road before taking a sharp left turn signposted with that most encouraging of invitations for the off-road cyclist – 'Unfit for cars'. A steep climb takes you up onto Mosser Fell and through outlying farms before another 'Unsuitable for motors' sign leads you east to Low Lorton. A tiny lane through Lorton Vale beneath the towering slopes of Gasgale Crags sets you up for the last off-road section and the final downhill through woodland back to the start.

Start

Lanthwaite Wood car park at the bottom of Scale Hill to the east of Loweswater, 10 km (6 miles) south of Cockermouth

P As above

Distance and grade

22 km (14 miles)

Easy / moderate

Terrain

Almost all the ride is on metalled surfaces. With the exception of a 800 m (½ mile) section in fields near the end, the off-road riding is on stone-based tracks. Three climbs: 122 m (400 ft) from Loweswater to the high point on Mosser Fell; 91 m (300 ft) from

Loweswater   Waterend   Mosser

Mosser Mains to the high point on Whin Fell; 70 m (230 ft) along the B5289 to the start of the last off-road section.
Highest point – 244 m (800 ft) on Mosser Fell.
Lowest point – 73 m (240 ft) at the crossing of the River Cocker near to Lorton

Nearest railway

Workington, 16 km (10 miles) west of the route at Waterend

Places of interest

The Lortons 8
Lorton Hall is partly a 15th-century peel tower, built as a refuge for the villagers against raiding Scots during the Border wars. The Jennings brewery in Cockermouth started off in what is now the village hall in High Lorton. At the rear stands a yew tree under which the founder of the Quaker movement, George Fox, preached pacifism to a large crowd that included Cromwellian soldiers. William Wordsworth in his poem Yew Trees wrote:

'There is a yew tree, pride of Lorton Vale
Which to this day stands single, in the midst
Of its own darkness, as it stood of yore'

Refreshments

Kirkstile Inn PH 🍴🍴, ***Loweswater***
*Coffee and tea at **the Grange Country House Hotel** (at the northern end of Loweswater)*
*Wheatsheaf PH, **Low Lorton** (just off the route)*

Low Lorton

Brackenthwaite

1 Exit Car Park turn L, cross bridge then 1st L 'Lowpark ½, Highpark ¾'

2 At T-j by Kirkstile Inn bear R (in effect SA) uphill. At T-j with road L then after 300 m (yd) at brow of hill 1st L 'Public Bridleway'

3 At fork of tracks bear R past small parking area. At fork of tracks in wood take either track – they link up. Climb to Hudson Place and bear R onto tarmac

4 At T-j with road opposite Grange Hotel R

5 After 1½ km (1 mile), in the wood, sharply L back on yourself 'Mosser. Unfit for cars'

6 Steep climb. Up over brow and down through Mossergate Farm. 400 m (¼ mile) after going through Mosser Mains 1st R over small stone bridge 'Unsuitable for motors'

7 At T-j R. Cross bridge. At T-j R then L 'Keswick 8½'

8 1st R at X-roads 'Hopebeck 1'

9 At T-j with B5289 L 'Buttermere 4, Loweswater 2' then 1st L 'Buttermere 4, Crummock Water'

10 Climb steadily through the wood. 400 m (¼ mile) after the end of the wood, just before house ahead, R through wooden bridlegate 'Public Bridleway'

11 Through gates continuing in same direction. At offset X-roads with more major track SA downhill. At T-j R to return to the car park

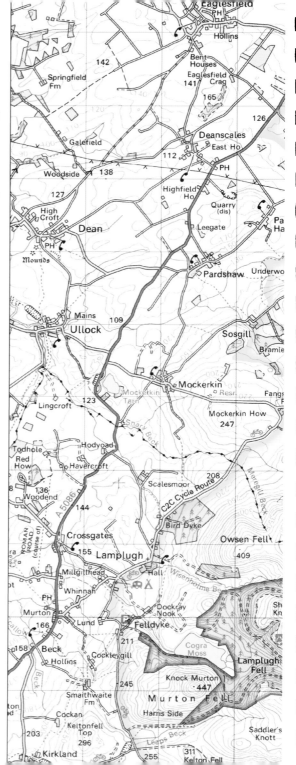

Two loops from Eskdale Green between Muncaster Fell and Wast Water

Between the sea and the western slopes of the high fells lies an area of farms and woodlands with fine views towards the high hills and a good quantity of fine bridleways. This ride describes a figure of eight with the two loops linking near to Santon Bridge, to the southwest of Wast Water. For convenience of parking, the route starts at Eskdale Green. Several short sections of bridleway are linked before a longer climb takes you east through forest setting up a fine descent, at first technical, then grassy back down to the road. It looks from the map as though there should be a good loop around the back of Wast Water but the author found this track too steep, rocky, boggy or vague. However, the detour alongside Wast Water to Wasdale Head is well worth making for the dramatic views and atmosphere of being at the very heart of the fells. The route continues in a southwesterly direction towards Muncaster Fell, which is almost encircled by the course of the route. There is a short rough/boggy section near to the miniature railway but the track on the southern side of the fell is superb all the way back to the start with fine views southeast to Ulpha Fell.

 Start

Irton Road Station, Eskdale Green (on the Ravenglass and Eskdale railway). Eskdale Green is off the A595 half-way between Whitehaven and Barrow-in-Furness

P As above

 Distance and grade

37 km (23 miles) (two loops of 18½ km (11½ miles))
🗲🗲🗲 Moderate

 Terrain

The tracks are predominantly stone-based but there may be some short pushing sections on the stretch through the forest on the northern part of the route. There is a 3 km (2 mile) section running alongside the Ravenglass railway that may be boggy in parts. 183 m (600 ft) climb

Eskdale Green

Santon Bridge

Whin Garth

from crossing the River Bleng near Hall Bolton to the top of the forestry section near Hollow Moor. 131 m (430 ft) climb from the railway to Chapel Hill on Muncaster Fell. Highest point – 231 m (760 ft) in the forestry at the northern end of the ride. Lowest point – 7 m (25 ft) south of Muncaster Fell

▲ Wasdale Head and Great Gable

Nearest railway

Ravenglass, 1½ km (1 mile) from the route at Muncaster Castle

Refreshments

Bower House Inn PH ●, George IV PH ●, **Eskdale Green**
Bridge Inn PH, **Santon Bridge**
Strands Hotel PH ●, The Screes PH ●, **Nether Wasdale**
Ratty Arms PH ●, **Ravenglass** (just off the route)

Places of interest

Ravenglass (just off the route) 26
Lies on an estuary where three rivers – the Esk, the Mite and the Irt – enter the sea, and for a long time its sheltered position made it an important harbour. The Romans used it and in the 2nd-century, built the large fort of Glannaventa on the cliffs above. In the 18th-century, Ravenglass was much used as a base for smuggling contraband tobacco and French brandy from the Isle of Man. The century-old miniature railway was once used to carry minerals and now takes tourists on a scenic 11 km (7 mile) trip up Eskdale

Muncaster Castle 26
Home of the Pennington family since the 13th-century, it was a sanctuary for Henry VI during the Wars of the Roses. There is an owl aviary and rhododendron gardens

Nether Wasdale

Santon Bridge

Watermill

Chapel Hill

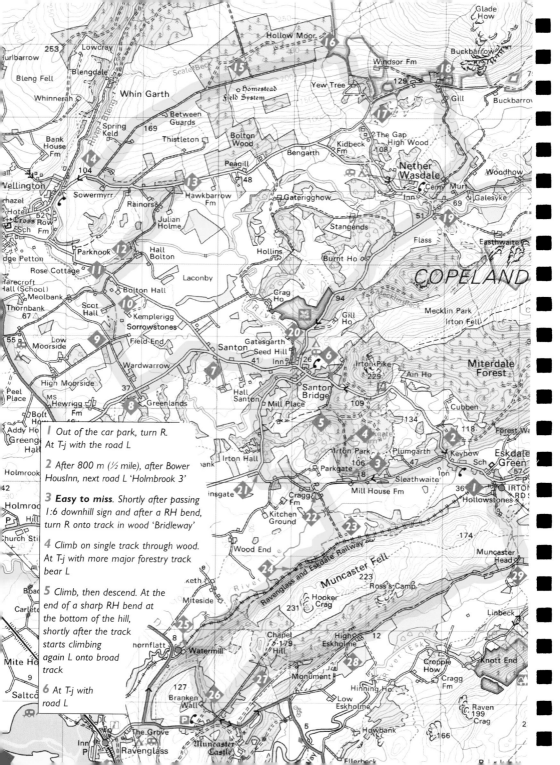

1 Out of the car park, turn R. At T-j with the road L

2 After 800 m (½ mile), after Bower Houslnn, next road L 'Holmbrook 3'

3 **Easy to miss**. Shortly after passing 1:6 downhill sign and after a RH bend, turn R onto track in wood 'Bridleway'

4 Climb on single track through wood. At T-j with more major forestry track bear L

5 Climb, then descend. At the end of a sharp RH bend at the bottom of the hill, shortly after the track starts climbing again L onto broad track

6 At T-j with road L

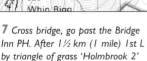

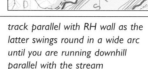

7 Cross bridge, go past the Bridge Inn PH. After 1½ km (1 mile) 1st L by triangle of grass 'Holmbrook 2'

8 After 1 km (¾ mile), shortly after wood starts on left 1st R onto driveway to Wardwarrow Farm 'Public Bridleway'

9 After 800 m (½ mile) 1st track R then after 100 m (yd) L onto grassy track along the edge of woodland

10 At T-j with better track bear R (in effect SA). Follow track as it swings R by house

11 At X-roads with road SA onto stone track 'Public Bridleway Hall Bolton, Bolton Head'

12 With cattle grid and houses ahead bear L downhill

13 Cross bridge, ignore turnings to left and right. At T-j with road L

14 After 1 km (¾ mile) at brow of hill R 'Public Bridleway. Cathow Bridge'

15 Steady climb over 3 km (2 miles) with forestry on one or both sides. Short sections where you will have to push

16 At the end of the wood where the walls spread out, cross stream via wooden bridge and follow grassy

track parallel with RH wall as the latter swings round in a wide arc until you are running downhill parallel with the stream

17 The track follows the RH wall as it swings L downhill to cross stream and become more distinct. Stony, technical descent becomes fast, grassy descent. At T-j with road L over cattle grid

18 After 800 m (½ mile) 1st track R 'Little Ground. Ghyll Farm'. At fork of tracks by gate bear L 'Bridleway'

19 At T-j with road R then L 'Santon Bridge 2, Drigg 6'. (**Or** turn L at road for thoroughly recom-mended detour along the edge of West Water to Wasdale Head)

20 At T-j after 3 km (2 miles) L 'Eskdale, Broughton 14' then 1st R 'Irton ¾, Ravenglass 5'

21 At brow of hill after 1½ km (1 mile), 1st road L by post box 'Eskdale Green 2½, Broughton 13½'

22 After 800 m (½ mile) at bottom of hill by collection of farm buidings turn R 'Sandbank. Public Bridleway'

23 Cross two fields. 100 m (yd) before hillside turn R alongside stone wall. Through gate at end of field and across next field in same

direction. From the gate at the end of this field diagonally L to a gate in the far LH corner

24 Follow railway line with the fence to your left. At times a rough push. Keep eye out for bridlegate to the L to cross tracks and continue in the same direction, with the line now to your right

25 At times narrow and muddy. It improves, becoming broad, stone track. Shortly after sign for 'Mill and Road' to the right sharply L back on yourself 'Bridleway. Castle'

26 Steep climb (push). Follow 'Bridleway' and 'Permitted Bridleway' signs for the castle. At X-roads of tracks beyond gate L uphill. At T-j with road sharply L back on yourself 'Public Bridleway. Muncaster Fell via Fell Lane'

27 **Easy to miss**. Shortly after brow of hill, leave main gravel track and take 1st grassy track to the R 'Public Bridleway. Lower Eskdale'

28 Fine descent. At T-j L

29 After 2½ km (1½ miles), with farm buildings to the left, turn L by fir trees. Follow past Forest How back to the start

5 *From Eskdale Green across to the Duddon Valley and back over Birker Fell*

An off-road ride that involves a sustained push of some forty minutes from the bottom of Hardknott to the top of the pass between the valleys of the rivers Esk and Duddon beneath Harter Fell. There is a chance to warm up for this with a 6½ km (4 mile) section of delightful, rideable off-road running parallel with the road and river, although there must be some sort of record for the number of gates that need to be opened along this stretch. The push climbs 259 m (850 ft) on a straightforward stony track, then across the roots of recently cleared forestry before joining a splendid forestry track that descends to the road running alongside the beautiful River Duddon. You may well be tempted by the attractions of the Newfield Inn at Seathwaite before girding your loins for the steep road climb up over Birker Fell and back down to the start.

Start

George IV PH, at the eastern end of Eskdale Green, 10 km (6 miles) east of Gosforth. (Gosforth is halfway between Whitehaven and Barrow-in-Furness on the A595)

P Go past George IV PH following signs for Ulpha and Broughton. Cross bridge. There is a large layby; just past the bridge on the right

Distance and grade

30 km (19 miles)
Strenuous

Terrain

The section alongside the River Esk is rideable. From the road at the bottom of Hardknott to the pass is mainly pushing on a well-defined stony track then across a short, rough stretch of cleared forestry. Two major climbs: 259 m (850 ft) from the road to the pass beneath Harter Fell, 192 m (630 ft) from Ulpha to the top of the road over Birker Fell. Highest point – 350 m (1150 ft) below Harter Fell. Lowest point – 24 m (80 ft) at the start

Nearest railway

Ravenglass, 10 km (6 miles) west of Eskdale Green

▲ *Seathwaite*

Places of interest

River Duddon Valley 10
Its magnificent scenery is immortalized by Wordsworth in no fewer than 35 individual sonnets. His poem 'Excursion' describes the village of Seathwaite and its 18th-century parson, Robert Walker

Ravenglass and Eskdale Railway 1
Established in 1875 to carry iron ore, this narrow gauge railway known as 'La'al Ratty' has been revived to carry passengers through 11 km (7 miles) of countryside between Dalegarth in Eskdale to Ravenglass on the coast

Refreshments

*George IV PH 🍺, Bower House Inn PH 🍺, **Eskdale Green**/ Newfield Inn PH 🍺, **Seathwaite***

Seathwaite

Ulpha

Birker Fell

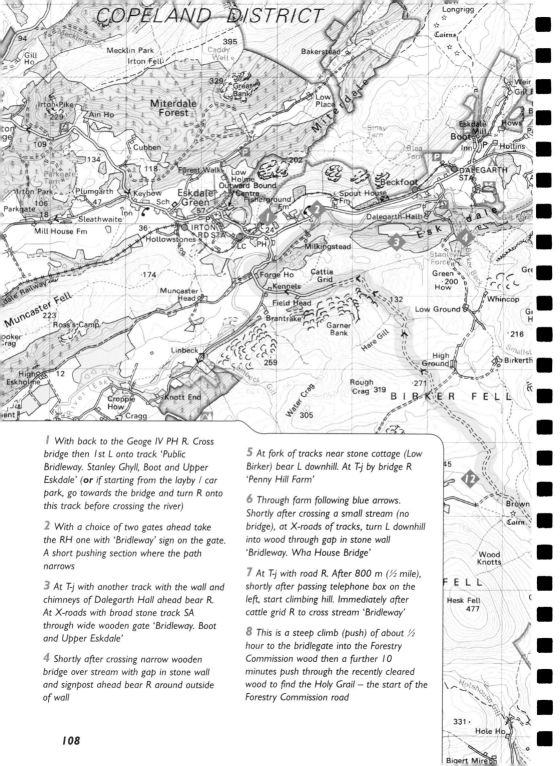

1 With back to the Geoge IV PH R. Cross bridge then 1st L onto track 'Public Bridleway. Stanley Ghyll, Boot and Upper Eskdale' (**or** if starting from the layby / car park, go towards the bridge and turn R onto this track before crossing the river)

2 With a choice of two gates ahead take the RH one with 'Bridleway' sign on the gate. A short pushing section where the path narrows

3 At T-j with another track with the wall and chimneys of Dalegarth Hall ahead bear R. At X-roads with broad stone track SA through wide wooden gate 'Bridleway. Boot and Upper Eskdale'

4 Shortly after crossing narrow wooden bridge over stream with gap in stone wall and signpost ahead bear R around outside of wall

5 At fork of tracks near stone cottage (Low Birker) bear L downhill. At T-j by bridge R 'Penny Hill Farm'

6 Through farm following blue arrows. Shortly after crossing a small stream (no bridge), at X-roads of tracks, turn L downhill into wood through gap in stone wall 'Bridleway. Wha House Bridge'

7 At T-j with road R. After 800 m (½ mile), shortly after passing telephone box on the left, start climbing hill. Immediately after cattle grid R to cross stream 'Bridleway'

8 This is a steep climb (push) of about ½ hour to the bridlegate into the Forestry Commission wood then a further 10 minutes push through the recently cleared wood to find the Holy Grail – the start of the Forestry Commission road

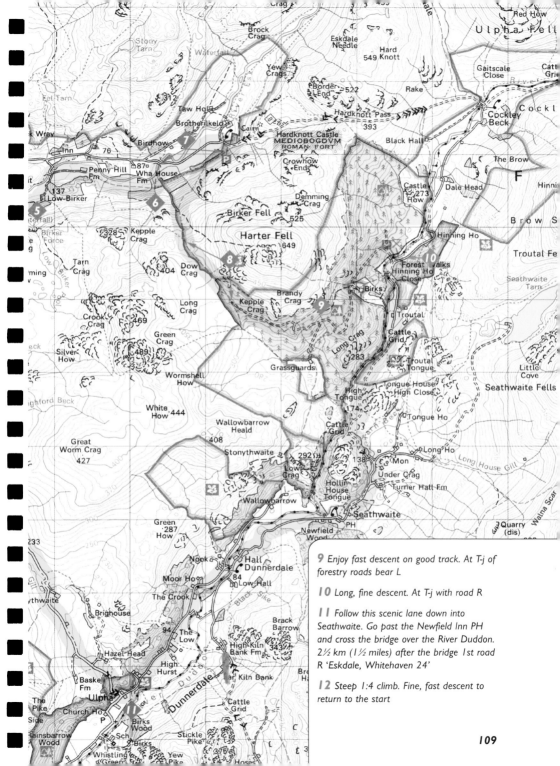

9 Enjoy fast descent on good track. At T-j of forestry roads bear L

10 Long, fine descent. At T-j with road R

11 Follow this scenic lane down into Seathwaite. Go past the Newfield Inn PH and cross the bridge over the River Duddon. 2½ km (1½ miles) after the bridge 1st road R 'Eskdale, Whitehaven 24'

12 Steep 1:4 climb. Fine, fast descent to return to the start

Sawrey and Claife Heights at the northwest corner of Lake Windermere

This is a small, perfectly formed ride that has most of the ingredients that one would ever wish to find in an off-road trip: good quality tracks with regular waymarking, rideable climbs and fast descents, wide-ranging views and a long flat off-road section by a lake to finish. All this and a bike-friendly ferry crossing of the lake to take you to the start of the ride. The ferry is a commercial concern running every fifteen minutes non-stop from morning to late evening and it is one of the greatest cycling pleasures to ride past the line of cars to get to the head of the queue. The ferry only takes five minutes and is cheap and easy to use. The route climbs from Far Sawrey up onto Claife Heights past three small tarns. From here, the views are magnificent. A fast forestry road drops you near to Wray Castle, from which point, there is a superb lakeside track running all the way back to the ferry. This ride could easily be linked to the signposted routes in the Forestry Commission land in Grizedale Forest.

Start

Car parks either side of the ferry from Bowness-on-Windermere

P Use the long-stay (slipway) pay and display car park on the way to the ferry at the south end of Bowness

Distance and grade

16 km (10 miles)
Easy

Terrain

Excellent tracks throughout. One steady 152 m (500 ft) climb from the start up onto Claife Heights. Highest point – 198 m (650 ft) near to Wise Een Tarn. Lowest point – Lake Windermere 42 m (140 ft).

▶ Lake Windermere

Far Sawrey

Wise Een Tarn

High Wray

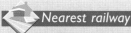

Nearest railway

Windermere, 4 km
(2½ miles) north of
the ferry at Bowness

Places of interest

Bowness 1
Resort on Lake Windermere with quaint,
narrow streets and 15th-century church. The
World of Beatrix Potter Exhibition
includes 3-D tableaux and videos

Hill Top, Near Sawrey 2
Scenes from Peter Rabbit come alive in the
17th-century farm that inspired Beatrix
Potter's work

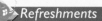

Refreshments

Plenty of choice in **Windermere** and
Bowness
The Sawrey Hotel PH 🍷, **Far Sawrey**

Three Dubs Crags

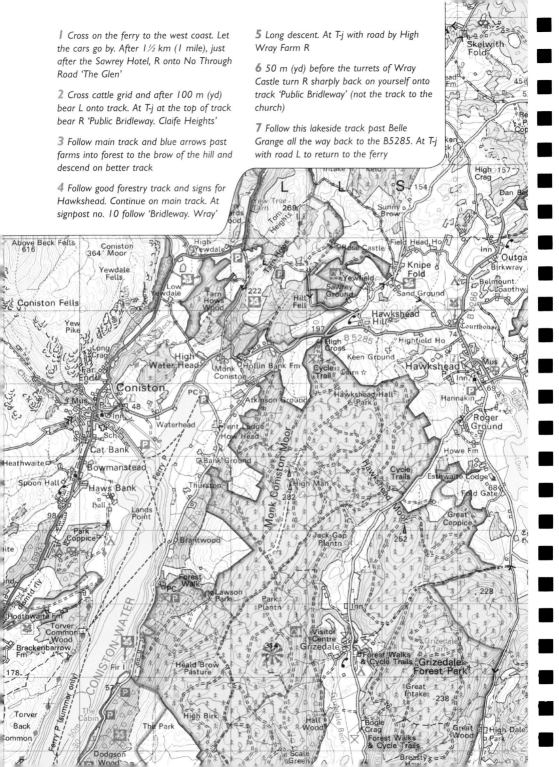

1 Cross on the ferry to the west coast. Let the cars go by. After 1½ km (1 mile), just after the Sawrey Hotel, R onto No Through Road 'The Glen'

2 Cross cattle grid and after 100 m (yd) bear L onto track. At T-j at the top of track bear R 'Public Bridleway. Claife Heights'

3 Follow main track and blue arrows past farms into forest to the brow of the hill and descend on better track

4 Follow good forestry track and signs for Hawkshead. Continue on main track. At signpost no. 10 follow 'Bridleway. Wray'

5 Long descent. At T-j with road by High Wray Farm R

6 50 m (yd) before the turrets of Wray Castle turn R sharply back on yourself onto track 'Public Bridleway' (not the track to the church)

7 Follow this lakeside track past Belle Grange all the way back to the B5285. At T-j with road L to return to the ferry

Tracks and green lanes east of Lake Windermere

*E*ast of Lake Windermere lies a tangled web of lanes, green lanes, old county roads, byways and bridleways that offer some very fine year-round cycling away from the seething hordes in the central fells. Heading south from Crosthwaite, the ride soon finds the delightful track that runs from Row in an arc west, then south beneath Whitbarrow. A climb up to Witherslack Hall is rewarded with a long, leisurely descent through woodland down to the road. Nothing so far

Start

The Punch Bowl PH, Crosthwaite, 8 km (5 miles) west of Kendal

P By the church at the eastern end of Crosthwaite

Distance and grade

38 km (24 miles) Moderate

Terrain

Almost all the route is on good quality tracks, many of which are unclassified roads that turn from tarmac to track with great frequency. 122 m (400 ft) climb from the River Gilpin south of Crosthwaite to the highest point of the bridleway beneath Whitbarrow. 213 m (700 ft) climb from the River Winster west of Witherslack to the the farm at Height. Highest point – 228 m (750 ft) on the road just beneath Gummer's How. Lowest point – 7 m (25 ft) at the crossing of the River Winster near to Witherslack

Nearest railway

Windermere, 6½ km (4 miles) north of the route near Winster

prepares you for the brutal, unrelenting climb up onto Newton Fell, a total of almost 210 m (700 ft) with the first 152 m (500 ft) within the first mile! Once gained, the height is more or less maintained on a series of unclassified roads running towards Gummer's How, then north towards Winster. Two excellent pubs lie just off the route at Strawberry Bank and Bowland Bridge, although this will involve losing some height. Green lanes, bridleways and tiny roads lead you back to the start at Crosthwaite.

Crosthwaite   Row   Park Wood   Witherslack   River Winster

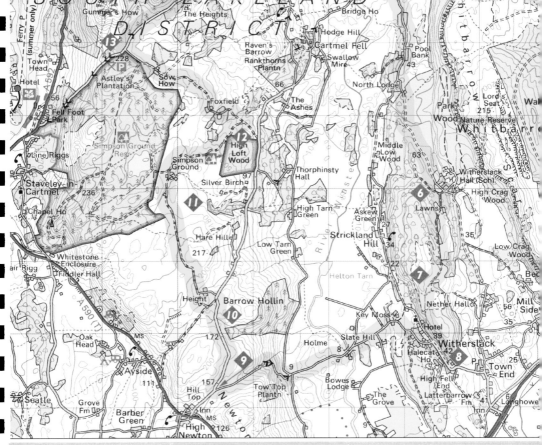

start on next page

6 After 4 km (2½ miles), at end of wood opposite large stone barn on left at brow of hill, R onto track 'Public Bridleway. Knot Wood, Halecat'. At fork by house bear R

7 At end of stone track bear R uphill away from the wall to the left on indistinct grassy track which soon becomes more obvious. Aim for gate in the middle of the far wall

8 Superb descent through woodland. At T-j with road sharply R back on yourself, then after 800 m (½ mile) 1st road L 'Newton, Cartmel Fell, Halecat'

9 Follow signs for High Newton up very steep hill. At T-j R 'Cartmel Fell, Kendal 12'

10 After short descent and climb 1st road L at top of hill (through gate) then 1st R 'Simpson Ground only'

11 At fork near to the house at Simpson Ground bear L uphill through gate. At end of tarmac bear R alongside wall 'Public Right of Way'

12 At T-j with tarmac L. Through farm (Foxfield) and onto track

13 Through next farm onto tarmac. At T-j with road R

next page

1 With back to the Punch Bowl PH L, then just past the Village Hall on the right L down track by village signboard and house called 'Oak Lea'

2 At T-j with road L then after 300 m (yd) R onto track through Esp Ford (near 'Aspen' sign) 'Public Bridleway'

3 At T-j with main road (A5074) L then after 1 km (¾ mile) 1st road R 'The Row'

4 Easy to miss. Through Row on tarmac lane which becomes track. Climb steadily, then descend. Track narrows as it runs along the side of the woodland to your left. Keep eye out for bridlegate to R in wall / fence into field and towards farm

5 Aim for the upper end of the farm. Descend on track through farm. At T-j with road L

⬅ *previous page*

14 Easy to miss. Fast descent. Once out of forest, opposite Lightwood Guest House on the right, L onto narrow road (NS)

15 At T-j L (NS)

16 Shortly after passing left turn to Low and High Moor How, with two road turns to the right in quick succession, take the 2nd R 'Bowness' then 1st R onto road between stone gate posts (NS)

17 Tarmac becomes track. As track swings sharp R towards farm and gate with 'Private' sign on it bear L onto grassy track and alongside wall. Through gate, keeping wall to your right and woodland to your left

18 At 'Ghyll Head' signpost R towards road. At X-roads with road SA '6 ft 6 ins width limit' onto track. At X-roads with next road SA 'Green Lane'

19 Tarmac turns to track. At T-j with road R (NS) then L (NS). Do not lose control!

20 On sharp LH bend by a sign for 'Crosthwaite' 1st R (in effect SA)

21 Follow in same direction towards barn with black doors. Bear L downhill then 1st R opposite house

22 Follow path alongside stream. At T-j by farm L then R onto road

23 At T-j after 2½ km (1½ miles) L to return to the start

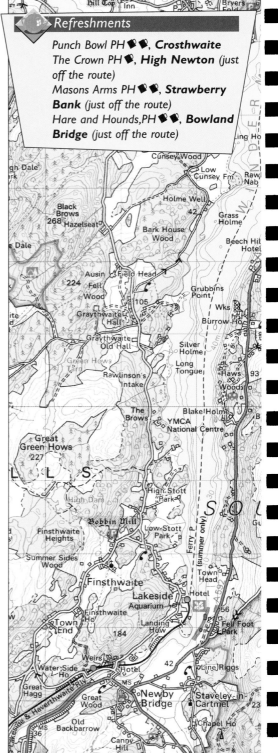

Refreshments

Punch Bowl PH🍺🍺, **Crosthwaite**
The Crown PH🍺, **High Newton** (just off the route)
Masons Arms PH🍺🍺, **Strawberry Bank** (just off the route)
Hare and Hounds, PH🍺🍺, **Bowland Bridge** (just off the route)

Burneside and the Garburn Pass between Kentmere and Troutbeck

Start

The Jolly Anglers PH, Burneside, 5 km (3 miles) north of Burneside

P No specific car park. Please park with consideration

Distance and grade

30 km (19 miles)
///// Strenuous

Terrain

There is a grassy section that is well signposted from Staveley Head Fell down into Kentmere. The track over Garburn Pass is

This ride involves a sustained push that lasts about half an hour from Kentmere to the top of the Garburn Pass. The reward is a long, fine descent with magnificent views of the central fells. Garburn Pass lies at the heart of the ride: at the start there is a steady climb alongside the River Kent from Burneside to Bowston and Hagg Foot and up over Staveley Head Fell past outlying farms before a fine descent down into Kentmere. The climb up to the Garburn Pass is straightforward on a stony track. A climb of 1½ km (1 mile) is compensated by a descent of almost 6½ km (4 miles) down to cross the busy A591, the road carrying most of the traffic into the heart of the Lakes. This main road is avoided in favour of quiet gated roads and a final green lane before the return to Burneside.

Burneside · Staveley Head Fell · Long Houses · Kentmere · Garburn Pass

stone-based, although the ascent is a push and there may be short sections on the descent where you need to walk. 192 m (630 ft) climb from Bowston to the top of Staveley Head Fell. 289 m (950 ft) climb from Kentmere to the Garburn Pass. Two climbs of 61 m (200 ft) to the south of the A591. Highest point – 457 m (1500 ft) at Garburn Pass. Lowest point – 51 m (170 ft) at the start

Nearest railway

Burneside

Refreshments

Jolly Anglers PH, **Burneside**

Places of interest

Troutbeck *(just off the route)* 12
This dispersed, picturesque settlement is worth visiting for its many surviving farmhouses and cottages, which are usually grouped around wells. The best conserved of them all is Townend, a 17th-century farmhouse now owned by the National Trust. Its interior decoration is uncommonly intact, with carved and dated fittings and furnishings. Dating and initialling was evidence of the Lakelanders' pride in their great prosperity after the mid-17th century, when their poor economy improved with cattle grazing and industrial sidelines in metals and stocking-knitting

Lake Windermere *(seen from the route)* 15
Windermere is a busy lake, with the resort town of Bowness-on-Windermere centrally located on its eastern shore. Steamers, yachts, pleasure boats and a chain ferry are some of the craft that can regularly be seen from the fells overlooking the lake. On the wooded Belle Isle, just opposite Bowness, a cylindrical mansion, built in 1774, pokes its roof up through the tree tops

Dubbs Reservoir

Heaning

New Hall

Rather Heath

1 With back to the Jolly Anglers PH R

2 After 1½ km (1 mile) 1st road R in Bowston (NS)

3 Ignore two road turns to the right and a bridleway to Mire Foot. Shortly after crossing a stream coming down the hillside from the right, next R 'Spring Hag Kennels'. At fork bear L following 'Kennel' signs

4 At junction of tracks by barn bear R 'Public Bridleway'

5 At X-roads with concrete track SA. At T-j with road R

6 At T-j by black metal barn ('Littlewood Farm' sign) L. At next T-j R

7 Past Low Fold and Park How. Go through large black metal gate 'Bridleway only' then after 100 m (yd) L through stone wall (blue arrow)

8 Follow grassy path, at times faint through gates marked with blue arrows. Track becomes stone-based and descends. At T-j with road R

Take care not to mistake the faded yellow line of the national park boundary for the solid yellow line of the route.

9 Follow tarmac road past church to its end ignoring right turn to Hartrigg Farm. At final house R steeply uphill on stony track 'Public Bridleway to Troutbeck via Garburn Pass'

10 You will need to push most of the way for about ½ hour to the top of the pass. There are short sections where you may also need to dismount on the descent

11 At fork shortly after wood on the left bear L on upper track

12 At T-j with road L

13 After 1 km (¾ mile) as descent steepens near to the bottom of the hill R towards farm buildings

14 Go past 1st farm. Just before second farm, on RH bend bear L onto grassy track. Bear L as better track joins from the right

15 At X-roads with main road SA **take care**

16 After 1 km (¾ mile) at fork of roads shortly after gate bear R uphill

17 At T-j L. Ignore left turn by cattle grid and left turn to The Glen. At bottom of hill, just as road starts to rise, take next L 'Dales Way'

18 Through several gates. At X-roads SA 'Ashes Farm. Gated green road'

19 At T-j with tarmac near to caravan park bear L

20 At next T-j R 'No exit to A591'

21 **With extreme care** cross A591, turn R then 1st L 'Burneside 1'

22 At T-j R to return to the start

West from Kirkby Stephen over the fells of Smardale and Crosby Garrett to Great Asby

9C

Start

Start of Silver Street (Soulby Road) Kirkby Stephen, 16 km (10 miles) east of M6, Junction 38

P Just off Silver Street (Soulby Road)

Distance and grade

36 km (22½ miles)

🚲🚲🚲🚲

Moderate/strenuous

Terrain

Well-drained earth / grass tracks over parts of Smardale and Crosby Garrett Fells and also west from Whygill Head. 228 m (750 ft) climb from

Between the Lake District and the Pennines, north of the Howgills and south of the Eden Valley lies an area of sparsel populated gently rolling fells with a plethora of bridleways where it is possible to plan several loops. This ride uses as a base the attractive town of Kirkby Stephen with lots of tea shops and pubs to look forward to upon your return. It climbs southwest over Smardale Fell crossing the lovely stone bridge over Scandal Beck. From Brownber, the route skirts the flanks of Nettle Hill before a reasonably good descent down to Crosby Garrett. The course of the ride lies westwards along grassy tracks from Whygill Head. Great Asby is a charming, unspoilt village and offers the only refreshment stop on the whole route. There is a last section of off-road before a 8 km (5 mile) stretch of the Cumbria Cycleway through Soulby and back to the start.

Kirkby Stephen   Waitby   Smardale Bridge   Brownber   Crosby Garrett

Kirkby Stephen to the top of Smardale Fell; 106 m (350 ft) from the crossing of Scandal Beck to the high point on Nettle Hill; 82 m (270 ft) climb from Water Houses west to Maisongill. Highest point – 335 m (1100 ft) on Smardale Fell. Lowest point – 152 m (500 ft) in Soulby

Nearest railway

Kirkby Stephen station lies 3 km (2 miles) south of the town

Refreshments

Kings Arms PH 🍺, White Lion PH 🍺, plenty of choice in Kirkby Stephen
Three Greyhounds PH, Great Asby

Places of interest

Kirkby Stephen 1
Brightly painted shops and old coaching inns huddle among attractive cobbled squares above the Eden valley. Inside the 13th-century St Stephen's church is the shaft of the unique 10th-century cemetery cross of Loki, the Danish Devil. The Market Square is surrounded by an ancient collar of cobblestones that mark the area used until 1820 for bull baiting – a sport that ceased after a disaster when a bull broke free

Crosby Garrett 11
Ancient records show that the village was once called Crosby Gerard, although no one seems to know who Gerard was! Crosby means farmstead with a cross. In the early days of Christianity, communities without churches made do with simple wood or stone crosses

Nettle Hill 11
Nettles had various uses including dye for local wool and are a sign of earlier human settlement. These hills are covered with cairns and hut circles

Great Asby

Soulby

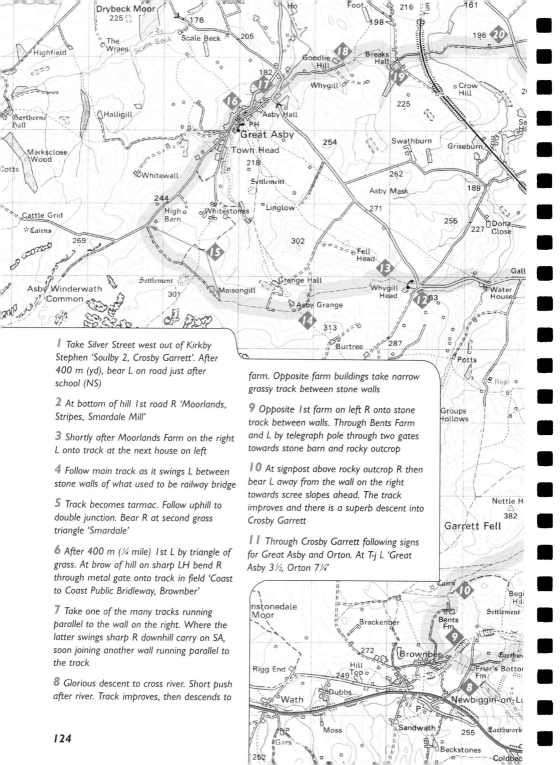

1 Take Silver Street west out of Kirkby Stephen 'Soulby 2, Crosby Garrett'. After 400 m (yd), bear L on road just after school (NS)

2 At bottom of hill 1st road R 'Moorlands, Stripes, Smardale Mill'

3 Shortly after Moorlands Farm on the right L onto track at the next house on left

4 Follow main track as it swings L between stone walls of what used to be railway bridge

5 Track becomes tarmac. Follow uphill to double junction. Bear R at second grass triangle 'Smardale'

6 After 400 m (¼ mile) 1st L by triangle of grass. At brow of hill on sharp LH bend R through metal gate onto track in field 'Coast to Coast Public Bridleway, Brownber'

7 Take one of the many tracks running parallel to the wall on the right. Where the latter swings sharp R downhill carry on SA, soon joining another wall running parallel to the track

8 Glorious descent to cross river. Short push after river. Track improves, then descends to farm. Opposite farm buildings take narrow grassy track between stone walls

9 Opposite 1st farm on left R onto stone track between walls. Through Bents Farm and L by telegraph pole through two gates towards stone barn and rocky outcrop

10 At signpost above rocky outcrop R then bear L away from the wall on the right towards scree slopes ahead. The track improves and there is a superb descent into Crosby Garrett

11 Through Crosby Garrett following signs for Great Asby and Orton. At T-j L 'Great Asby 3½, Orton 7¼'

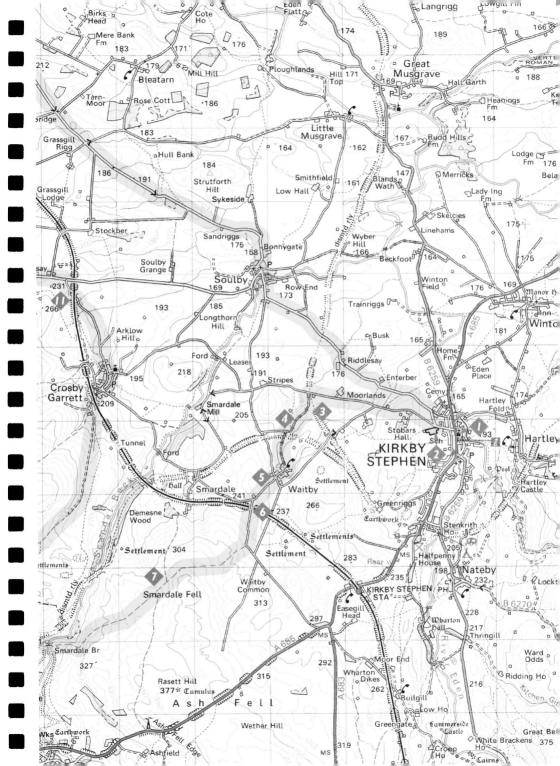

Notes

Notes

Useful addresses

British Cycling Federation
National Cycling Centre
Stuart Street
Manchester M11 4DQ
0870 871 2000
www.bcf.uk.com

The BCF co-ordinates and promotes an array of cycle sports and cycling in general. They are a good first point of contact if you want to find out more about how to get involved in cycling. The website provides information on upcoming cycle events and competitions.

CTC (Cyclists Touring Club)
Cotterell House
69 Meadrow
Godalming
Surrey GU7 3HS
01483 417217
www.ctc.org.uk

Britain's largest cycling organisation, promoting recreational and utility cycling. The CTC provides touring and technical advice, legal aid and insurance, and campaigns to improve facilities and opportunities for all cyclists. The website provides details of campaigns and routes and has an online application form.

The London Cycling Campaign
Unit 228
30 Great Guildford Street
London SE1 0HS
020 7928 7220
www.lcc.org.uk

The LCC promotes cycling in London by providing services for cyclists and by campaigning for more facilities for cyclists. Membership of the LCC provides the following benefits: London Cyclist magazine, insurance, legal advice, workshops, organised rides, discounts in bike shops and much more. You can join the LCC on its website.

Sustrans
Head Office
Crown House
37-41 Prince Street
Bristol BS1 4PS
General information line: 0117 929 0888
www.sustrans.org.uk

A registered charity, Sustrans designs and builds systems for sustainable transport. It is best known for its transformation of old railway lines into safe, traffic-free routes for cyclists and pedestrians and wheelchair users. Sustrans is developing the 13,000 km (8000 mile) National Cycle Network on traffic-calmed minor roads and traffic-free paths, to be completed by the year 2005 with major funding from the Millennium Commission.

Veteran Cycle Club
Membership Secretary
31 Yorke Road
Croxley Green
Rickmansworth
Herts WD3 3DW
www.v-cc.org.uk

A very active club, the VCC is concerned with the history and restoration of veteran cycles. Members enjoy organised rides and receive excellent publications relating to cycle history and club news.